BUSINESS ENGLISH

BY

THE EDITORIAL STAFF

OF

THE DONALD PUBLISHING CO., INC.

MONARCH
PRESS

TENTH PRINTING, 1985

Published by
MONARCH PRESS
a Simon & Schuster division of
Gulf & Western Corporation
Simon & Schuster Building
1230 Avenue of the Americas
New York, N.Y. 10020

Standard Book Number: 0-671-18128-9

Printed in the United States of America

FOREWORD

The business world today is, of course, unbelievably immense. It reaches from the smallest shop on the next street corner to the giant corporations with their branches all over the world. Literally millions and millions of people are now continuously engaged, day in and day out, in correspondence among the various units that make up this tremendous organization. Business letters, personal notes, contracts, inter-office communications are just a few of the hundreds of forms which this correspondence takes.

One of the keys to advancement and success in this great world of business is a knowledge of correct English. Whether you are still only a student or whether you are already working in some company, you must be able to express yourself in clear and concise English if you wish to succeed and get ahead.

This book will provide you with simple explanations of the various grammatical principles which govern the writing of correct English. Extensive drill exercises will help you to establish these principles firmly in your mind so that their usage becomes automatic.

The subject matter of the book covers the various parts of speech: noun, pronoun, verb, adjective, etc. These are presented here, however, not from a strictly grammatical point of view but rather from the standpoint of practice and usage. The explanations are given in simple, everyday language. There is a minimum of technical terminology. The drill exercises are similarly based on everyday materials. Most of the drill sentences are taken from current business correspondence.

Special sections are devoted to words frequently misused, to proper style in sentence composition, to the avoidance of corrupt or vulgar forms. A long and detailed section of almost forty pages, covering all phases of punctuation, completes this very comprehensive study of everyday, practical Business English.

The clear organization of the book should make it very easy for anyone to follow. The continuous mixture of practice exercises with basic grammar theory serves to lighten the general tone of the book, also makes it interesting, as well as practical, for both students and teachers to use.

TABLE OF CONTENTS

LESSON 1: THE SENTENCE 1

  1. Parts of a Sentence 1
  2. Sentence Fragments 3
  3. Run-On Sentences 6
  4. Agreement of Subject and Predicate 8
  Exercises 14

LESSON 2: NOUNS 18

  1. Types of Nouns 18
  2. Capitalization of Proper Nouns 19
  3. Forming Plural Nouns 22
  4. Possessive Nouns 25
  Exercises 27

LESSON 3: PRONOUNS 30

  1. The Forms of Pronouns 30
  2. Possessive Pronouns 30
  3. The Relative Pronouns 31
  4. Pronouns and Their Antecedents 32
  Exercises 35

LESSON 4: VERBS 38

  1. Types of Verbs: Action and Linking 38
  2. The Simple Tenses 40

3. The Progressive Form 41
4. The Perfect Tenses 42
5. Summary of Tenses 46
6. Verb Forms 47
7. Regular and Irregular Verbs 48
8. Verbs and Objects of Verbs 52
9. Lie and Lay—Sit and Set—Rise and Raise 53
10. If I were 57
Exercises 58

LESSON 5: ADJECTIVES 67

1. Comparison of Adjectives 67
2. Using Adjectives 69
3. Articles 72
4. Repeating the Article 73
Exercises 73

LESSON 6: ADVERBS 79

1. Forming Adverbs 79
2. Choosing Between Adverbs and Adjectives 80
3. Using Adverbs 81
Exercises 84

LESSON 7: PREPOSITIONS 88

1. Using Prepositions 89
2. The Right Preposition 90
Exercises 92

LESSON 8: MORE ABOUT PRONOUNS 97

1. Types of Pronouns 97
2. Using Pronouns 100
3. Who—Whom 101
4. Whoever and Whomever 104
Exercises 105

LESSON 9: CONJUNCTIONS 112
   1. Using Conjunctions 112
   2. Interjections 113
   Exercises 113

LESSON 10: PUNCTUATION 115
   1. The Period 115
   2. The Question Mark 116
   3. The Exclamation Point 117
   4. The Comma 117
   5. The Colon 126
   6. The Semicolon 127
   7. Quotation Marks 128
   8. The Apostrophe 130
   9. The Hyphen 131
  10. The Parentheses 133
  11. The Dash 133
  12. Capitalization 134
   Exercises 136

LESSON 11: WORDS FREQUENTLY CONFUSED 152
   Exercises 160

COMMON ABBREVIATIONS 165

THE SENTENCE

Let's assume that one sunny afternoon your doorbell rings. You answer it and this is what you hear from the gentleman standing on your doorstep:

"Acme Company. Super Champion. Cleaner."

What would you do? You would probably slam the door in his face.

Instead, assume this is what you hear:

"How do you do. I represent the Acme Company, maker of the world-famous Super Champion vacuum cleaner."

Very probably you would ask to hear more about the Super Champion.

This is not intended to be a lesson in salesmanship. It is a lesson in communication.

In the above example, both salesmen had ideas they wished to convey to you. Salesman No. 1 spoke in a garbled, incoherent manner. The door was slammed in his face. Salesman No. 2 spoke in composed, clear sentences. He may make the sale.

Communication is the mainspring of action. If you don't want the door slammed in your face you must learn to communicate in a clear, coherent manner. You must learn to say what you mean, and say it in a way that others will understand. You must learn to compose your thoughts into complete sentences that express exactly what you have in mind, and leave no room for confusion.

1. The Parts of a Sentence

We say that you must speak in complete sentences. Let's start with the basic question: *What is a sentence?* You know that a sentence is a group of words. But more than that, it is a group of words that expresses a *complete thought*. This is very important, as you shall soon see. Remember, every sentence must express a *complete thought*.

To express a complete thought, every sentence must include two parts:

1. Someone or something to talk about;

1

2. Something to say about that person or thing.

You may remember from your grammar-school days that we call the part of the sentence that tells us *whom* or *what* we are talking about the *subject* of the sentence. The name we give to the part of the sentence that tells us what that person or thing *does* is the *predicate* of the sentence.

In outline form, therefore, every sentence must contain two parts:

1. *A subject:* which tells us whom or what we are talking about;
2. *A predicate:* which tells us what the subject does.

John speaks.

This is a complete sentence. It tells us:

1. Who? **John.** (The subject)
2. Does what? **Speaks.** (The predicate)

Tall, handsome John speaks.

This too is a complete sentence. We have merely added some words which describe our subject. *They do not change the subject.* The subject is still **John** and the predicate is still **speaks.**

Tall, handsome John speaks with fluency and persuasion.

Again, this is a complete sentence. **Tall, handsome** describes **John**. **With fluency and persuasion** describes **speaks**. The subject remains **John**. The predicate remains **speaks**.

Use this approach whenever you want to find the subject and the predicate of a sentence. Just ask yourself two simple questions:

a. Whom or what are we talking about? (The subject)
b. What does the subject do? (The predicate)

Disregard all other words which merely describe the subject and the predicate.

EXAMPLES:

1. **The manager works with diligence and initiative.**
   a. Who? **Manager.** (The subject)
   b. Does what? **Works.** (The predicate)
      Disregard, **with diligence and initiative.**

2. On Wednesday evening, after the banquet, the executives will meet.
   a. Who? **Executives.** (The subject)
   b. Do what? **Will meet.** (The predicate)
   Disregard, **On Wednesday evening, after the banquet.** . . .
3. **Stand still!**
   a. Who? **You.** (Understood)
   b. Do what? **Stand.**
   Disregard, **still.**

What do we mean by *understood?* This is a particular type of sentence—a command. Most commands are given quickly and curtly. The subject of the command is taken for granted to mean *you.* Remember, though, in all other types of sentences the subject must be specifically stated. Only in commands can the subject be left to the imagination.

2. Sentence Fragments
Is this a sentence?

John.

Obviously not. It names a subject, **John,** but does not tell us what the subject *does.* In other words, it is not a sentence because it contains no predicate.
Is this a sentence?

Tall, handsome John.

Again, the answer is, *No.* Our subject is described to us, but we are still not told what he does. We still have no predicate. Remember, a sentence must contain both a subject and a predicate, and it must express a complete thought. A frequent mistake that some secretaries make is to write only part of a sentence as though it were a complete sentence.

For example:

WRONG: **John Smith, president of our firm. Was invited to the banquet.**

Is either of these parts a complete sentence?

   1. **John Smith, president of our firm.**
   2. **Was invited to the banquet.**

No. Neither part is a complete sentence. Part 1 contains a subject, but no predicate. Part 2 contains a predicate, but no subject. Alone, each part is merely a *fragment* of a sentence. The good secretary corrects all sentence fragments. *Guard against sentence fragments!*

To correct sentence fragments like 1 and 2, above, is simple.

Right: John Smith, president of our firm, was invited to the banquet.

We now have one sentence that includes a subject and a predicate and expresses a complete thought.

EXAMPLES:

1. **Right:** Our book, the latest, most authoritative word on the subject, has just been put on the market

    Wrong: Our book, the latest most authoritative word on the subject. Has just been put on the market.

2. **Right:** The course that we are offering you is the finest you can get anywhere.

    Wrong: The course that we are offering you. Is the finest you can get anywhere.

There is another type of sentence fragment of which you should beware on the job. This is the fragment which apparently contains both a subject and a predicate but does not express a complete thought.

For example, is this a sentence?

John, running at full speed.

Let's test it.

1. Who? **John.** (The subject)
2. Doing what? **Running.** (The predicate)
3. Complete thought? NO! It leaves us with the question: **John running at full speed** *what?* This sentence fragment can be corrected as follows:

John, running at full speed, fell.

Remember, a sentence must express a complete thought! If it does not express a complete thought it is not a sentence, it is merely a fragment of a sentence. Beware of sentence fragments:

EXAMPLES:
1. **Right:** Our firm, having written to you last month, expected a reply by now.

   Wrong: Our firm, having written to you last month. Expected a reply by now.

2. **Right:** He looked about and saw people running in all directions.

   Wrong: He looked about and saw people. Running in all directions.

3. **Right:** Knowing the situation as I do, I advise against it.

   Wrong: Knowing the situation as I do. I advise against it.

Now let's turn to the final type of sentence fragment. Is this a complete sentence?

Since the order arrived.

Answer: NO! The word **since** limits our thought in such a manner that it does not express a complete thought although it contains a subject, **order,** and a predicate, **arrived.** The expression **since the order arrived** leaves you up in the air. You want to know:

Since the order arrived, *what happened?*

You must add something to complete the thought. For example, you might say:

Since the order arrived, we have made headway.

The expression, **since the order arrived,** is called a *dependent clause.* It cannot stand by itself. The word **since** makes it *dependent* upon the main thought, **we have made headway.** There are many small words like **since,** that limit a thought, render it incomplete by itself, and make it *dependent* upon a main thought. For example:

1. **Though we received your order, we could not fill it.**
   (The word **though** makes **though we received your order** incomplete by itself. It makes it *dependent* upon the main thought, **we could not fill it.**)

5

2. **As soon as** we heard the news, we ran to congratulate you.
(As soon as makes as soon as we heard the news *dependent* upon we ran to congratulate you.)

3. We left the theater **because** we failed to get the part.
(Here, the dependent part comes last. **Because** makes because we failed to get the part *dependent* upon we left the theater.)

4. We kept trying, **until** it was too late.
(**Until** makes until it was too late, *dependent* upon we kept trying.)

As a secretary, you must never write one of these dependent expressions by itself, as though it were a complete sentence.

Wrong: **Since the order arrived.**

This is not a complete sentence. It is merely a fragment of a sentence. Guard against sentence fragments!

EXAMPLES:

1. **Right:** **Though the weather was cloudy, we went sailing.**
   WRONG: Though the weather was cloudy. We went sailing.

2. **Right:** **Although we received your last shipment, we feel it is of such inferior quality that we should not pay.**
   WRONG: Although we received your last shipment. We feel it is of such inferior quality that we should not pay.

3. **Right:** **He won because he was the fastest.**
   WRONG: He won. Because he was the fastest.

3. Run-On Sentences

Look at these two sentences:

1. **We hope to attend the banquet.**
2. **We may be detained by business.**

You could combine these two sentences into one thought, as follows:

3. **We hope to attend the banquet, but we may be detained by business.**

Don't you agree that Sentence 3 better expresses the ideas of Sentences 1 and 2?

Very often you will have two sentences that are so closely related that you may want to combine them into one. However, don't think that you can throw them together in a haphazard fashion. A sentence is like a building block. To connect two building blocks, you would use a good ·strong glue. To attach one sentence to another, you also need a strong *glue* to hold them together. This *glue* is supplied in Sentence 3 by the word **but**.

> 3. **We hope to attend the banquet, <u>but</u> we may be detained by business.**

As you will learn in Lesson Nine, the word **but** is called a *conjunction*. Two other conjunctions that can be used as *glue* to hold sentences together are **and** and **or**. For example:

> **Mr. Jackson took the 5:15 train, <u>and</u> he should be here any minute.**
> **You must accept our offer, <u>or</u> you will suffer the consequences.**

One great mistake that you should always avoid is to try to attach two sentences without using a strong enough *glue*. Here are two examples of the use of *glue* that is too weak to do the job.

> 1. Wrong: **We hope to attend the banquet we may be detained by business.**
>   (Here no *glue* is used at all. There is nothing to hold the two sentences together. They fall apart.)
> 2. Wrong: **We hope to attend the banquet, we may be detained by business.**
>   (Here a comma is used to hold the two sentences together. But a comma is not a strong enough *glue* to do the job. The two sentences again fall apart.)

These two sentences are examples of an error that we call the *Run-On Sentence*. When two sentences are thrown together without a strong enough *glue* to hold them, the result is a run-on sentence. To correct such run-on sentences, either separate the two parts into separate sentences, or use a strong *glue* like **but, and, or.**

7

Right: We hope to attend the banquet, but we may be detained by business.

You have probably guessed that the run-on sentence is the opposite of the sentence fragment. The run-on sentence contains too much while the sentence fragment does not contain enough. Both are equally undesirable. Remember these points, then:

1. To connect two sentences you must use a strong *glue* such as the conjunction **and, but, or.**
2. You cannot hold two sentences together by using no *glue* at all or by using only a comma as *glue.*

EXAMPLES:

1. Right: Here is your order. We look forward to your reply.
   Right: Here is your order, and we look forward to your reply.
   WRONG: Here is your order we look forward to your reply.
   WRONG: Here is your order, we look forward to your reply.
2. Right.   We are new in this field. Our clocks are unmatched in quality.
   Right: We are new in this field, but our clocks are unmatched in quality.
   WRONG: We are new in this field our clocks are unmatched in quality.
   WRONG: We are new in this field, our clocks are unmatched in quality.

4. Agreement of Subject and Predicate

When you answer your boss' phone, you would never say, "Mr. Smith are here." You wince just to think of it. However, when sentences are more complicated, you may fall into just such an error, and that is where knowing the subject and predicate can help you on the job.

For your sentence to be grammatically correct, *its predicate must agree with its subject in number.* This means that if the subject is singular, you use a singular predicate. If the subject is plural, you use a plural predicate.

For example, what would you do with a sentence like this?

One man in this firm of hundreds (is, are) to be honored.

To solve this problem merely ask yourself: What is the subject of this sentence? Who is to be honored? **One man** is to be honored, not **this firm of hundreds.** Since the predicate must agree with the subject in number, use the singular predicate **is.** The sentence now reads:

8

One man in this firm of hundreds is to be honored.

Below is a series of hints to help you determine whether to use a singular or a plural predicate.

Hints on Agreement of Subject and Predicate.

HINT 1.

Jack and Jill (is, are) going up a hill.

This problem-sentence is easy. It contains two subjects (**Jack, Jill**) connected by **and**. The sentence means that both of them are going up a hill. So it calls for the plural predicate **are**.

Jack and Jill are going up a hill.

This is the general rule: Whenever a sentence contains two or more subjects connected by **and,** use a plural predicate.

> **The Acme Company and the Omega Company are merging.**
> **Good bookkeepers and good stenographers are hard to find.**

There is, however, one exception to this rule. When both subjects really refer to one person or one thing, use a singular predicate. For example:

The treasurer and secretary is here.

One man holds both posts. *He* is here. However, if the posts are held by two different men, then the general rule applies:

The president and the secretary are here.

But:

Bread and butter is a fine food.

Bread and **butter** are so closely identified as to be considered one unit. Therefore, use the singular predicate, **is**

HINT 2.

Jack or Jill (is, are) going up the hill.

In this problem, notice first that there are two subjects connected by **or**, **Jack or Jill**. Here's a little trick that will help you with sentences like this when you are a secretary. Whenever two subjects are connected by **or** or **nor**, make the predicate agree with the subject *closer* to it.

Jack or Jill (is, are) going up the hill.

Jill is closer to the predicate. **Jill** is singular. Therefore, use the singular predicate, **is**.

1. **Jack or Jill is going up the hill.**
2. **Either Mr. Jones or Mr. Smith is going to the meeting.**
   (**Mr. Smith** is closer to the predicate. **Mr. Smith** is singular. Therefore use the singular predicate, is.)
3. **Neither the chair nor the table has arrived.**
   (Remember, the same rule applies to two subjects connected by **nor**. **Table** is closer to the predicate. **Table** is singular. Therefore, has.)
4. **The boys or the girls are going to win.**
   (**Girls** is closer to the predicate. **Girls** is plural: Therefore, use the plural predicate, **are**.)
5. **Neither the chairs nor the tables have arrived.**
   (**Tables** is closer to the predicate. **Tables** is plural. Therefore, use have.)
6. **Either the secretaries or their bosses are to blame.**
   (**Bosses** is closer to the predicate. **Bosses** is plural. Therefore, use are.)
7. **Mr. Sawyer or his sons (has, have) studied your problem.**
   (This sentence is a little more complicated. One of the subjects is singular, **Mr. Smith**. The other subject is plural, **sons**. By applying our general rule, we can easily determine the proper predicate. **Sons** is closer to the predicate. **Sons** is plural. Therefore we use the plural predicate, have.)

Mr. Sawyer or his sons have studied your problem.

HINT 3.

Words such as **each, anybody,** and **nobody** are tricky. You can save yourself a great deal of grief on the job if you remember that when any one of the following words is the subject of a sentence, you use a *singular* predicate.

1. **Each. Each of the officers in the firm is a future chairman.**
   (The subject is **each,** not **officers. Each** means **each** *one.* Therefore, use the singular predicate, **is.**)
2. **Anyone. Anyone is qualified for the job.**
   (**Anyone** means **any** *one,* and is therefore singular.)
3. **Anybody. Anybody is capable of filling this position.**
   Anybody is the same as **any** *one,* and is therefore singular.)
4. **Someone. Someone is going to suffer for this.**
   (**Someone** means **some** *one.*)
5. **Somebody. Somebody has missed the point.**
   (**Somebody** is the same as **some** *one.*)
6. **Everyone. Everyone in Brooklyn was sad when the Dodgers lost.**
   (**Every** *one* was sad.)
7. **Everybody. Everybody wants to go to the meeting.**

HINT 4.

When determining the subject disregard expressions beginning with words such as **of, in, at.** These small words are called *prepositions.* In Lesson 6 we will discuss prepositions at length. For now, just remember that you disregard an expression that begins with a word such as **of, in,** or, **at** when looking for the subject of a sentence. Look at these examples.

1. **Each of the soldiers is a potential leader.**
   (Disregard **of the soldiers. Each . . . is a potential leader.**)
2. **Nobody in the whole army is capable of doing a better job.**
   (Disregard **in the whole army. Nobody . . . is capable of doing a better job.**)

HINT 5.

Always disregard expressions beginning with **as well as, together with,**

in addition to, *etc.*

1. **The book, as well as the papers, has been received.**
   (The subject is **book**. Disregard, **as well as the papers**.)
2. **My employer, in addition to his associates, was pleased.**
   (The subject is **employer**. Disregard, **in addition to his associates**.)
3. **Mr. Smith, together with his secretary, is scheduled to arrive at noon.**

HINT 6.

In determining whether a subject is singular or plural always look to the *meaning* of the word rather than its form. For example, take the word **news**. Though **news** ends in **s** it is singular in meaning. Therefore it calls for a singular predicate.

> **No news is good news.**
> **The news is encouraging.**

Similarly, though the word **series** ends in **s**, it too is singular.

> **The series of revisions is completed.**
> **A series of changes has been made.**

Finally the names of a number of school subjects and diseases end in **s** but are singular in meaning. For example: **Economics, politics, civics, physics, mathematics, measles,** and **mumps.**

> **Economics is a required subject, as is civics.**
> **Measles is a mild disease.**

HINT 7.

When a quantity is measured in *one lump sum* it should be treated as though it were one item. For example:

1. **Five tons is a lot of coal.**
   (We are really referring to one large amount of coal.)
2. **Eighty miles per hour is too fast.**
   (80 miles per hour is one speed.)
3. **Two hundred dollars is a fair amount.**
   (We are referring to one sum of money.)

On the other hand, when a quantity is measured in *piece-by-piece* units, use a plural predicate.

> **There are five men waiting.**
> **In this box are eighty shirts.**
> **Two hundred units have been produced.**

You may have trouble when the word **number** is the subject of a sentence. Remember this rule-of-thumb: When **number** is preceded by the, use a singular predicate. When any other word, including **a**, precedes **number**, use a plural predicate.

> **The number of failures is low.**
> **A number of people have failed.**

HINT 8.

Beware of titles of books and articles that sound plural. For example:

1. **Right:** **"Business Letters" is a fine book.**
   You are referring to one book, though its title sounds plural.
2. **Right:** **"Notes on Fashions" is in this issue of Jones Magazine.**
   This is one article. Therefore, use the singular predicate.

HINT 9.

There are a few words that are either singular or plural, depending upon their meaning in a sentence—words such as **committee, jury, class, crowd,** and **army.** Each of these words refers to a group of people. When that group acts as a *single* unit, use a *singular* predicate.

> **The committee is in session.**
> **The class is meeting in the room.**

However, when you refer to the *individuals* that make up the group use a *plural* predicate.

> **The committee are in disagreement.**
> **The class were arguing with one another.**

Exercise 1

Subject and Predicate

This problem deals with identifying the subject and the predicate of a sentence. In each of the following sentences, underline the subject with one line; underline the predicate with two lines. Remember, ask yourself two questions: 1. Who or what? (The subject) 2. Does what? (The predicate) Disregard all other words.

1. I like this book.

2. This book has been sold to over 200,000 readers.

3. These readers have uniformly expressed their delight with this book.

4. Did you enjoy it too?

5. I certainly did enjoy it.

6. Jack and Jill went up a hill.

7. Mr. Roberts and Mr. Jones are in their office.

8. At the stroke of noon the President and his cabinet met in the East Wing.

9. Have you seen the President and his cabinet in session?

10. Neither Mr. Black nor Mr. Green has sent in his reply.

11. We wish to see either Miss White or Miss Brown.

12. Neither of them is here.

13. She can type and file expertly.

14. The secretary has transcribed and mailed the letter.

Exercise 2

Sentence Fragments

This problem deals with recognizing incomplete thoughts. As you know, a sentence must express a complete thought. Below is a list of expressions. Some of them express complete thoughts. In the space provided mark C next to these sentences to indicate that they are *complete* sentences. The rest of these expressions do not express complete thoughts. Mark F next to these to indicate that these expressions are sentence *fragments*.

1. Running down the street at full speed.   1. __F__

2. Despite his lack of experience and maturity.   2. ____

3. We agree.   3. ____

4. Night after night, day after day, till he could hardly speak anymore.   4. ____

Exercise 2 (continued)

5. Mr. Roberts, the most noted authority on aerodynamics in recent years.   5. _____

6. Furtively looking up and down the street, then darting to safety in the shadows,
   he escaped.   6. _____

7. Where are we going?   7. _____

8. Despite all his protestations to the contrary and his insistence that he was inno-
   cent, he was convicted.   8. _____

9. Although we were certain that he was a fine leader and were willing to follow
   him wherever he would lead.   9. _____

10. When the order arrives and is processed by the receiving department.   10. _____

11. Despite explicit orders to the contrary.   11. _____

12. Nearing the attainment of the production goals set at our last meeting.   12. _____

13. Nearly everyone present, including the President and his aides.   13. _____

14. Nearly everyone was present, including the President and his aides.   14. _____

15. There is no time for further discussion.   15. _____

Exercise 3

Run-on Sentences

This problem deals with recognizing run-on sentences. Some of the following sentences
are correct; others are run-on sentences. Rewrite the run-on sentences correctly in the space
provided. Mark C in that space if the sentence is correct.

1. Have your representative call, a definite appointment should be made in advance.

   Have your representative call. A definite appointment should be made in advance.
   _____

2. Maybe later on we will be willing to do as your order man writes, just now, however, we do
   not wish to change.

   _____

   _____

3. Are the letters and articles graded according to difficulty, in our book they are.

   _____

   _____

4. Mr. James Quinn, a man with considerable experience in office planning, will be ready to help
   you on March 4.

   _____

   _____

5. However, just now we do not wish to change, we are sure you will understand.

_____

6. But read the booklet, yours will bear your imprint on the front and back covers.

_____

7. She learns all the good points and fortifies herself with facts and evidence about the superiority of York Silk and the weak points of others, so that when she is ready to buy silk she will want York and no other.

_____

Exercise 4
Sentence Fragments and Run-on Sentences

A. This problem deals with distinguishing a complete sentence from a sentence fragment or a run-on sentence. In the space provided, mark C if the expression is a complete sentence; mark F if it is a sentence fragment; and mark R if it is a run-on sentence.

1. Whenever the attorney had a chance to speak.   1. __F__
2. Ship the books, we will remit within 30 days.   2. _____
3. Lessons by day, study at night.   3. _____
4. Because of his initiative, and because he had the proper connections.   4. _____
5. What will happen next?   5. _____
6. Continue with your college course, you will graduate at the head of your class.   6. _____
7. Looking around, sizing up the situation, and foretelling all its ramifications.   7. _____
8. Oil, steel, and coal in the right proportions.   8. _____
9. Expect only big things of yourself, and never waver nor doubt that they will come true.   9. _____
10. While Miss Blake is young, she is not immature, so I am convinced she can handle the job.   10. _____

B. The letter below contains a number of sentence fragments and run-on sentences. Rewrite this letter, correcting all such faults in sentence structure.

Dear Mr. White:

No two men are alike, one man jumps to a conclusion without careful consideration of all available information. Another man examines each fact. Checks every claim. And profits from the experience of others, then he makes his decision.

Although we should like to aid you. You have not cooperated with us thus far. You can check in your own home. Each point and every claim that we make.

Mail the enclosed card today, we will ship a sample to your home by return post.

Sincerely yours,

Exercise 5

Agreement of Subject and Predicate

This problem deals with agreement of subject and predicate. In the space provided write the correct predicate. Remember, first find the subject; then choose its predicate. If you have any trouble, review the Hints on Agreement of Subject and Predicate.

1. Each order (has, have) been received.   1. _____has_____

2. Each of the orders (has, have) been received.   2. _____

3. Anyone (know, knows) what the solution should be.   3. _____

4. Walter Clark of Chicago, as well as his entire family, (intend, intends) to spend his summer here.   4. _____

5. Either Mr. Burns or Mr. Jones (is, are) the logical candidate.   5. _____

6. Somebody in the crowd (is, are) going to be surprised.   6. _____

7. One million dollars (is, are) a lot of money.   7. _____

8. We feel that neither your office nor your plants (is, are) adequately equipped.   8. _____

9. The committee (has, have) issued a final decree.   9. _____

10. Each of the children, in addition to his parents, (is, are) entitled to a free pass.   10. _____

11. A number of photos (were, was) taken.   11. _____

12. Anybody with a sound mind (are, is) eligible to enter.   12. _____

13. I feel that politics (has, have) entered a decade of decision.   13. _____

14. The number of books available for sale (are, is) low.   14. _____

15. Our prices and our workmanship (speak, speaks) for themselves.   15. _____

16. The foremen or the workmen (are, is) going to have to accept the responsibility.   16. _____

17. Hundreds of teachers, together with their students, (hail, hails) our product.   17. _____

18. Measles (is, are) a contagious disease.   18. _____

Lesson 2

NOUNS

Now that we have studied the sentence, let's turn to the words that make up the sentence. The names of most of these words are probably vaguely familiar to you: **nouns, pronouns, verbs, adjectives, adverbs, conjunctions,** and **prepositions.** You undoubtedly met most of these terms in your earlier schooling. On the other hand, you may have forgotten the exact meaning of these technical terms. Don't let that worry you!

Our purpose is to make you into a top-notch secretary. So, we shall start from the very beginning and leave nothing to chance.

You may wonder: "Why must they plague me with technical terms like **nouns,** and **verbs,** and the like?" And that's a good question. We could have omitted all such terms and given them other, simpler names. We could have called **nouns,** *name words,* and called **verbs,** *action words.* But would you really have gained by this? Probably not. More likely you would have become confused by the mixture in your mind of the new terms we would invent and those commonly-used terms you vaguely remember from grammar school.

So, rather than invent new terms for you to learn, we shall use the old familiar terms. If you don't remember them from your grammar-school days, that's no problem. We'll teach you all about them. If you happen to remember these terms, all the better. We'll reinforce what you already know, and teach you more.

Let's start with the words known as **nouns.**

1. The Types of Nouns

Nouns are *name words.* We use nouns to *name* persons, places, things, or abstract qualities.

Person	Place	Thing	Abstract Quality
man	city	chair	truth
stenographer	school	shorthand	initiative
president	lake	book	readiness

You can divide all nouns into two classes: **common nouns** and **proper**

18

nouns. A common noun names a *general* class of people, places or things. A proper noun names a *specific* person, place, or thing. Look at these paired examples:

Common Noun:	boy	country	car
Proper Noun:	John Jones	America	Pontiac

2. Capitalization of Proper Nouns

Did you notice that all the proper nouns listed above begin with capital letters?

John Jones   America   Pontiac

It's for this reason that learning to recognize proper nouns is important. Whenever you write a proper noun you must be sure to capitalize the initial letter. Proper nouns are essential to the American system of free enterprise. Every company name, every product name, every trade name is a proper noun. The business material you will handle on the job will be filled with proper nouns. So study the *Hints* listed below. They will help you solve the capitalization problems that you will face when you take office dictation.

Hints on Capitalization of Proper Nouns.

HINT 1.

Always capitalize the names of months of the year and days of the week.

Classes begin the first **Monday** in **February.**

HINT 2.

Never capitalize the names of the seasons.

Our **fall** order was not delivered until **winter.**

HINT 3.

Should you capitalize the name of a direction such as **east** or **west?**

a. When the name of a direction refers to a section of the country or the world, it should be capitalized.

The **West** is solid in its opposition to Communism.
The **Southwest** was once the land of cowboys and Indians.
The Mississippi flows through the **North** and the **South.**

Peru is in **South America.**

b. When a direction is used to refer to a point on the compass, it should NOT be capitalized.

The plane circled twice then headed **west.**
The Mississippi flows from **north** to **south.**
Philadelphia is **southwest** of New York.
Peru is **south** of Panama.

HINT 4.

Should you capitalize a geographic term such as **river, ocean, mountain,** or **valley?** The answer depends upon how you are using such a term. Learn these three simple rules.

a. Capitalize a geographic term, such as **river,** when you use it as part of the name of a *particular* river, or other geographical designation:

Hudson River
Pacific Ocean
Bear Mountain
Mohawk Valley

b. Do not capitalize a geographic term such as **river** when it is placed *before* the name of the river:

The river Hudson
The valley of the river Nile.

EXCEPTION: The word **mount** is capitalized even when it precedes the name of the mountain.

Mount Everest
Mount Rainier
Mount Whitney

c. Do not capitalize a geographic term such as **river** when you use it in the plural.

Missouri and Mississippi rivers
Atlantic and Pacific oceans
Appalachian and Rocky mountains

HINT 5.

Should you capitalize a word such as **hotel, highway, tunnel,** or **revolu-**

tion? Generally, capitalize such a word when you are using it as part of a proper name:

> New Yorker Hotel
> Lincoln Highway
> Holland Tunnel
> French Revolution

But:

> French and American revolutions
> New Yorker and Pennsylvania hotels

HINT 6.

Are titles such as **president, treasurer** or **director** capitalized? The rule preferred is:

a. Always capitalize the title of a person when it appears *directly* before or after the name of the title-holder.

> President Johnson will see you now.
> Send the message to John Johnson, President of the Acme Steel Company.
> We received the letter from James Roberts, Assistant Director of the Zenith Oil Company.

b. Generally capitalize the title of a *high-ranking* officer even when his name does not appear in the sentence.

> The Senator will return soon.
> The President was not at the White House.

c. There is some disagreement about whether the title of a less important office-holder should be capitalized when his name does not appear in a sentence. The preferred business practice is to capitalize such titles. After all, you express your respect for a person when you capitalize his title.

> The Director called the meeting to order.
> The letter is from the Superintendent of our Wyoming plant.
> The Secretary of our firm will be pleased to attend the dinner.

HINT 7.

Capitalize the first letter of each important word in the title of a work of art or literature. Do not capitalize unimportant words, such as **to, and, the,** which occur in the middle of the title.

21

Have you read "How to Win Friends and Influence People"?
Washington's Farewell Address was his greatest speech.
He entitled his talk, "Russia, the Modern Dilemma."
Have you ever seen the painting, "The Blue Boy"?

3. Forming the Plural of Nouns

Nouns, as you know, may be either singular or plural.

Singular	Plural
book	books
valley	valleys
tomato	tomatoes
radio	radios

Do you know how to spell plural nouns correctly? How do you spell the plural of **attorney?** of **solo?** of **brother-in-law?** As a secretary you will have to be able to spell these plural nouns properly at all times. Remember, WHEN IN DOUBT, LOOK IT UP! Use your dictionary. Most dictionaries include a special note under each noun showing the proper spelling of the plural of that noun.

But, you should not be in doubt too frequently. You should commit to memory the plural forms of most frequently-used nouns. To help you do this we have listed some rules to guide you.

These rules for forming plurals are not difficult. All they require is a little of your concentration.

RULE 1.

To form the plural of most nouns simply add *s*.

receipt	receipts	town	towns
piece	pieces	crowd	crowds
cigarette	cigarettes	desk	desks
group	groups	paper	papers

RULE 2.

To form the plural of a noun that ends in the sound *s, sh, x,* or *ch*, add *es*.

gas	gases	lash	lashes
glass	glasses	church	churches
bush	bushes	lunch	lunches
tax	taxes	box	boxes

RULE 3.

To form the plural of a noun that ends in *y* preceded by a vowel (*a, e, i, o, u*) simply add *s* to form its plural.

attorney	attorneys	trolley	trolleys
valley	valleys	play	plays

RULE 4.

To form the plural of a noun that ends in *y* preceded by a consonant (any letter other than *a, e, i, o, u*) change the *y* to *i* and add *es*.

baby	babies
company	companies
lady	ladies

RULE 5.

To form the plural of a noun that ends in *o* preceded by a vowel, merely add *s*.

portfolio	portfolios
radio	radios
patio	patios

RULE 6.

To form the plural of a noun that ends in *o* preceded by a consonant, add *es*.

tomato	tomatoes	potato	potatoes
cargo	cargoes	hero	heroes

EXCEPTIONS: Note that most of the exceptions are musical terms.

solo	solos
piano	pianos
soprano	sopranos
zero	zeros

RULE 7.

To form the plural of many nouns that end in *f*, change the *f* to *v* and add *es*.

half	halves	shelf	shelves
knife	knives	leaf	leaves
thief	thieves		

23

BUT NOTE:

chief	chiefs	handkerchief	handkerchiefs
proof	proofs	belief	beliefs
roof	roofs		

RULE 8.

Certain nouns have special foreign plural forms. Below is a list of the most frequently used ones. Try to learn to recognize these words.

basis	bases	criterion	criteria
crisis	crises	datum	data
thesis	theses	medium	media
alumna (female)	alumnae	memorandum	memoranda
alumnus (male)	alumni	phenomenon	phenomena

RULE 9.

Certain old English nouns have irregular plural forms. You should find these words familiar.

ox	oxen	child	children
man	men	woman	women

RULE 10.

When a compound noun is written as one solid word, without a hyphen, form the plural by making the last part plural.

bookcase	bookcases	classmate	classmates
courthouse	courthouses	letterhead	letterheads
workman	workmen	grandchild	grandchildren
stockholder	stockholders		

RULE 11.

When forming the plural of a compound noun that is written with a hyphen, make the principal part plural.

editor-in-chief	editors-in-chief
mother-in-law	mothers-in-law
brother-in-law	brothers-in-law
father-in-law	fathers-in-law
sister-in-law	sisters-in-law

Rule 12.

Form the plural of letters and numbers by adding 's.

h's	o's	2's	9's
g's	u's	7's	5's

4. Possessive Nouns

Another type of noun you will use frequently in business is the *possessive*. A possessive noun is one which shows ownership, authorship, or origin:

> Jack's book.
> Shakespeare's play.
> The lamp's glow.

The rules for spelling of possessive nouns were quite complicated at one time. In those awful bygone days you had to be a genius to know whether to add apostrophe *s* or just apostrophe to the name **Charles** or **Roberts**. Today, fortunately, these complicated rules are no longer followed. In fact, the modern rules for forming possessive nouns are extremely simple and will cause you no trouble on the job.

Rule 1.

Form the possessive of a noun that does not end in *s* by adding 's.

company	company's	hero	hero's
box	box's	child	child's
man	man's	children	children's
men	men's	John	John's

Note that it does not matter if the noun is singular or plural. If it does not end in *s*, add 's.

Rule 2.

Form the possessive of a noun that ends in *s* by adding an apostrophe only. Again, note that the rule applies whether the noun is singular or plural.

companies	companies'	grass	grass'
boxes	boxes'	Charles	Charles'
heroes	heroes'	Mr. Roberts	Mr. Roberts'

Hints on Forming Possessive Nouns

Hint 1.

A problem arises when you want to show joint ownership. How would you write this phrase in possessive form?

> **The operetta by Gilbert and Sullivan** . . .
>
> Answer: **Gilbert and Sullivan's operetta** . . .

To show joint possession, write only the last name in possessive form.

> **Smith and Miller's firm**

This means *one* firm owned jointly by Smith and Miller.

> **Johnson and Johnson's bandages** . . .
>
> **Rodgers and Hammerstein's play** . . .

But, when you want to show separate possession of distinct items write the name of each owner in possessive form.

> **Smith's and Miller's firms are strong competitors.**

This refers to two firms, one owned by Smith and the other by Miller.

> **New York's and Chicago's police forces are among the finest.**

This refers to the police force of each city separately.

Hint 2.

To write the possessive form of an abbreviation, place the apostrophe *s* (*'s*) after the final period.

> **The U.S.A.'s tariff** . . . **The U.N.'s policy** . . .

Hint 3.

To form the possessive of a compound expression, place the apostrophe *s* (*'s*) after the last word in the expression.

> **My brother-in-law's inheritance** . . . . (One brother-in-law)
>
> **My brothers-in-law's inheritance** . . . . (More than one brother-in-law)

Exercise 6

Proper Nouns

A. This problem involves capitalization of proper nouns. In the sentences below, some words that should be capitalized, are not capitalized. Other words that should not be capitalized, are capitalized. Cross out all incorrect letters and write the correct form above each.

1. The Medlock tool co. appreciates the Information it received from you on october 17.

2. Our Local board of education requests bids on the new School

3. The Boardman vocational institute has a new superintendent, samuel Jones.

4. Allen and white, inc. received your Order for the Fall line early in September.

5. Mr. Robert c. Phillips, chairman of the Firm of Phillips and sons, intends to open up the west as its newest market.

6. the Carlsbad hotel is located South of Main street.

7. The Advertising Agency of Bemis, Baumer, and Beard offers exceptional coverage throughout the northwest.

8. We have inquired of our Attorney, mr. john I. dowings, to ascertain our Rights against the Omega insurance co.

9. The assistant director of The Lakeland hotel is john doe, jr.

10. The president left the white house by Limousine at Noon and rushed to the airport.

Exercise 7

Plural Nouns

A. Write the plural form of each of these nouns in the space provided. Column A is listed in the order that the principles are presented in the text. Column B is in a random order.

Column A	Column B
1. book books	1. crisis
2. invoice	2. proof
3. office	3. bus
4. mass	4. box
5. tax	5. roof
6. match	6. laboratory
7. facility	7. handkerchief
8. colony	8. series
9. body	9. shelf
10. journey	10. thesis

11. attorney _____
12. studio _____
13. hero _____
14. embargo _____
15. echo _____
16. wife _____
17. half _____
18. chief _____
19. plaintiff _____
20. proof _____

11. watch _____
12. receipt _____
13. company _____
14. self _____
15. datum _____
16. radio _____
17. stimulus _____
18. valley _____
19. alumnus _____
20. criterion _____

B. This problem deals with recognizing improperly spelled plural nouns. In the following paragraph, ten plural nouns are improperly spelled. Cross out each incorrectly spelled noun and write the correct form above it.

Industries

~~Industrys~~ of all sorts have flourished in the central vallies of the Acme Mountains. Each year, cargos of tomatos and potatoes are shipped from the valleys in large quantities. The area is famous for its fine tobaccoes, which are bought by all the large cigar companys. In addition to these agricultural products the region has fine facilitys for steel foundrys and for the manufacture of radioes and pianoes.

C. This problem deals with recognizing plural nouns. Choose the proper predicate in each of the following sentences. Remember, if the subject is singular, use a singular predicate. If the subject is plural, use a plural predicate.

1. The data (has, have) been entered in the account book.
2. Our most successful media (is, are) radio and TV.
3. Our curriculum (include, includes) courses in many fields.
4. The bases for my contention (is, are) twofold.
5. (Were, was) the memoranda left on my desk?
6. The alumni (is, are) fully behind the dean.
7. The stimulus (has, have) been measured in electrical units.
8. The fathers-in-law (has, have) met for the first time.
9. The crisis in his illness (is, are) finally past.
10. The series of revisions (is, are) complete, at last.

1. _____have_____
2. _____
3. _____
4. _____
5. _____
6. _____
7. _____
8. _____
9. _____
10. _____

Exercise 8

Nouns—Plural and Possessive

This problem tests what you have learned about the spelling of possessive nouns and plural nouns. Fill in the form of the noun called for in each column—singular possessive, plural, and plural possessive.

Singular	Singular Possessive	Plural	Plural Possessive
1. book	book's	books	books'
2. child			
3. tax			
4. Smith & Smith			
5. wife			
6. ratio			
7. body			
8. criterion			
9. attorney			
10. workingman			
11. radio			
12. memorandum			
13. brother-in-law			
14. hero			
15. stockholder			
16. roof			
17. journey			
18. letterhead			
19. committee			
20. county			

Lesson 3

PRONOUNS

The pronoun is the efficient man's tool. It is a shortcut by which you can save time and space. How? The job of the pronoun is to stand in place of a noun. Since most nouns are long and most pronouns are short, you can shorten statements by skillfully using pronouns. Compare the lengths of the following sentences:

WITHOUT PRONOUNS	WITH PRONOUNS
The Coca Cola Bottling Company announced that the Coca Cola Bottling Company intends to double the sale of the Coca Cola Bottling Company's product.	The Coca Cola Bottling Company announced that it intends to double the sale of its product.

1. The Forms of Pronouns

Pronouns take different forms, depending upon how they are used in a sentence. You have used these different forms automatically for most of your life, so they should cause you no difficulty now.

	Singular	Plural
First Person (The person speaking)	I	We
Second Person (The person spoken to)	You	You
Third Person (The person spoken about)	He, she, it	They

These forms are familiar to you, aren't they? Then let's move on to another topic—the possessive form of pronouns.

2. Possessive Pronouns

You learned in the previous section that the possessive form of a noun is generally formed by adding an apostrophe *s* ('*s*). For example.

firm	firm's
author	author's
John	John's
America	America's

Now, look at the possessive form of these pronouns:

	Singular	Plural
First Person:	my, mine	our, ours
Second Person:	your, yours	your, yours
Third Person:	its, his, her, hers	their, theirs

What is the first thing you noticed about these possessive pronouns? That's right! You noticed that *none* of these possessive pronouns is written with an apostrophe. If you learn nothing else about pronouns, learn this one simple rule: The possessive pronouns, **yours, hers, its, ours** and **theirs** are written *without apostrophes*.

As an added warning, remember: The word **its** is a pronoun. The word **it's** is NOT a pronoun. **It's** is a contraction for the word **it is.**

For example:

It's illegal to sell liquor on Sunday.
(*It is* illegal to sell liquor on Sunday.)
The book lay on its side.
(The book lay on the book's side.)

It's going to be a cold winter.
The firm is proud of its history.
The officers say that it's not going to be sold.
How can your company increase its sales?

3. The Relative Pronouns: Who, Which, That

The words **who, which,** and **that** are another type of pronoun. They are used to *relate* one thought to another. For this reason they are called *relative* pronouns.

Look at these examples. Do you see how the relative pronoun in each sentence *relates* one thought to another?

Here is the man who will be our next president.
The book, which had fallen, was soon found.
The lion is the animal that I like best.

When should you use **who, which,** or **that?** The answer is simple:

1. Use **who** to refer to a person;
2. Use **which** to refer to an animal or a thing;
3. Use **that** to refer to a person, an animal, or a thing.

At one time there were complicated rules controlling the choice of **which** or **that**. Fortunately, today they may be used interchangeably to refer to an animal or a thing.

4. Pronouns and Their Antecedents

England expects every man to do (her) (their) (his) duty.

How do you know which pronoun to use? Let's work this problem through together. You remember that the function of the pronoun is to replace a noun. We call the noun that is replaced by the pronoun, the *antecedent* of that pronoun.

David says he is tired. (David is the antecedent of he.)
Mary knows she cannot succeed. (Mary is the antecedent of she.)
We have heard from our salesmen. They write that they cannot fill the quota. (Salesmen is the antecedent of they.)

Since a pronoun must stand in place of its antecedent, it should be as similar to the antecedent as possible. If the antecedent is singular, the pronoun must be singular. If the antecedent is masculine, the pronoun must be masculine.

Now, let us return to our problem sentence:

England expects every man to do (her) (their) (his) duty.

First, what is the antecedent? Right! The antecedent is **man**. Is the antecedent male or female? The antecedent, **man**, is clearly masculine. So we can eliminate **her** from our choice. Our problem is reduced to:

England expects every man to do (their) (his) duty.

The final step is to determine whether the antecedent is singular or plural. The antecedent, **man**, is singular. Therefore, we should use the singular pronoun, **his**.

Our sentence should read:

England expects every man to do his duty.

Once you learn to recognize antecedents you will never have trouble choosing the proper pronouns. The problem of agreement of a pronoun with its antecedent is very much like a problem you have already studied—the agreement of a subject and its predicate. Right now, go back to the section on agreement of subject and predicate and review all the hints given there. Only when you have fully refamiliarized yourself with that topic should you proceed with the hints given below on agreement of pronouns with their antecedents.

Hints on Agreement of Pronouns with their Antecedents.

HINT 1.

Try this sentence. It should be easy.

Jack and Jill are on (his, their) way.

Obviously, **their** is correct. The antecedent of **their** is **Jack and Jill.** Always use a plural pronoun to represent two or more antecedents connected by **and.**

Mr. Johnson and Miss Smith are on their way here.

The Acme Company and the Ajax Company are merging their assets.

HINT 2.

When two antecedents are connected by **or** or **nor,** have the pronoun agree in number with the *nearer* antecedent.

1. **Neither Johnson nor Smith knows his business.**
   (Smith is the nearer antecedent. Smith is singular. Therefore, use **his.**)
2. **Either Miss Smith or Miss Black will get her wish.**
   (Miss Black is the nearer antecedent. Miss Black is singular. Therefore, use **her.**)
3. **Neither the boys nor the girls are ready for their lessons.**
   (Girls is the nearer antecedent. Girls is plural. Therefore, use **their.**)
4. **Neither Mr. Smith nor his sons did their best.**
   (Sons is the closer antecedent. Sons is plural. Therefore, use **their.**)

HINT 3.

Remember, the following words are all singular: **each, every, everyone, everybody, someone, somebody, no one, nobody.** Therefore, each of these words, when used as an antecedent, calls for a singular pronoun.

> **Somebody** got up and gave **his** seat to an elderly woman.
> **Nobody** is willing to endanger **his** life unnecessarily.
> **Everyone** does **his** work efficiently.
> NOT: Everyone does *their* work efficiently.

HINT 4.

Which pronoun do you use in the following sentence?

> **Everyone in the class did (his) (her) homework.**

Is **everyone** masculine or feminine? It could be either. In such a case, where the sex of the antecedent is unknown, generally use a *masculine* pronoun. For example:

> **Not a person left his seat before the last curtain.**
> **One of the students left his cigarettes.**

HINT 5.

Always disregard a phrase beginning with **as well as, in addition to,** and **not.**

1. **John, as well as his brothers, is on his way.**
   (The antecedent is **John.** Disregard brothers.)
2. **The boys, in addition to John, are on their way.**
   (The antecedent is **boys.** Disregard John.)
3. **John, and not his brothers, is on his way.**
   (The antecedent is **John.** Disregard brothers.)

HINT 6.

Words like **committee, jury, class, crowd,** and **army** may be either singular or plural, depending upon their meaning in the sentence. Each of these words refers to a group of people. When you are referring to that group as a single unit, use a single pronoun.

The committee is holding its meeting.
The class is in its room.

However, when you refer to the individuals that make up the group use a plural pronoun.

The committee have announced their disagreement.
The jury brought in their split verdict.

Exercise 9

Possessive Pronouns

A. This problem deals mainly with the possessive forms of pronouns. In the space provided write the proper word. Remember, you do not write possessive pronouns with apostrophes. Choose the proper word and write it in the space provided.

1. The book fell on (its) (it's) side.   1. _____its_____

2. (Its) (It's) going to be a cold winter.   2. _____

3. The package on top is (ours) (our's).   3. _____

4. They claimed the package was (theirs) (there's) (their's).   4. _____

5. These men are certain (their) (they're) correct.   5. _____

6. Mr. Jones is a man (who) (which) can get his own way.   6. _____

7. Victory is (our's) (ours).   7. _____

8. The pact must stand or fall on (its) (it's) merits.   8. _____

9. (Yours) (Your's) truly,   9. _____

10. Here is the man (that) (which) I told you about.   10. _____

11. Our magazine has increased (its) (it's) circulation threefold. 11. _____

12. This car of (ours) (our's) is similar to (yours) (your's).   12. _____

_____

13. The school sent (its) (it's) catalogue to our principal.   13. _____

14. Mr. Smith and his colleagues have submitted (his) (their) (there) report.   14. _____

Exercise 10

Pronouns—Antecedents and Number

In this problem you are to identify the pronouns and their antecedents. In the column marked *Pronoun* write the pronoun. In the column marked *Antecedent* write the antecedent. In the column marked *Number* write S if the antecedent is singular, or write P if the antecedent is plural.

	Pronoun	Antecedent	Number
1. The present equipment deserves all the praise given it.	1. it	equipment	S
2. Mr. Jones is certain of his grounds.	2. _____	_____	___
3. The Acme Laundry knows it can count on continued community support.	3. _____	_____	___
4. The boy's rackets were hung on their sides.	4. _____	_____	___
5. Mr. Jones can protect his rights if he acts quickly.	5. _____	_____	___
6. Our firm is proud of its record.	6. _____	_____	___
7. Somebody forgot his glasses.	7. _____	_____	___
8. Each of the players has his part.	8. _____	_____	___
9. Mr. Jones and Mr. Smith are on their way to the meeting.	9. _____	_____	___
10. Mr. Jones, as well as Mr. Smith, is on his way to the meeting.	10. _____	_____	___
11. Each man must do his very best.	11. _____	_____	___
12. The committee has been in its meeting room for hours.	12. _____	_____	___

Exercise 11

Agreement of Pronoun and Antecedent

This problem deals mainly with the agreement of a pronoun with its antecedent. In the spaces provided write the proper pronouns.

1. Smith and Jones has grown till (it, they) is the largest firm in (its, it's, their) field.

   1. <u>it</u>
   <u>its</u>

2. If somebody does an outstanding job (he, they) will be rewarded for (his, their) efforts.

   2. _____
   _____

3. The memoranda (is, are) in (its, their) proper place.

   3. _____
   _____

4. Every girl in that class knows (his, her, their) lessons.

   4. _____

5. The crisis (is, are) over but has left (its, their) mark.

   5. _____
   _____

6. Now is the time for all good men to come to the aid of (his, their) country.

   6. _____

7. Each good man should come to the aid of (his, their) country.

   7. _____

8. No one in this world is certain of (his, their) future; yet each must plan as best (he, they) can.

   8. _____
   _____

9. If a man does a valiant deed (he, they) shall be adored wherever (he, they) goes.

   9. _____
   _____

10. Somebody tried to force (his, their) way through the crowd.

    10. _____

11. If Miss Smith or Miss Jones orders at once (she, they) will receive the merchandise by return post.

    11. _____

12. Either Mr. Dunlap or Mr. Firestone left (his, their) lighter.

    12. _____

13. Every man, woman, and child owed (his, their) life to the Coast Guard.

    13. _____

14. Neither Mr. Williston nor Mr. Blackstone was certain of (his, their) facts.

    14. _____

15. James Randall is the one man who realizes (his, their) value.

    15. _____

Lesson 4

VERBS

Verbs are the words in a sentence that pack the wallop. They give a sentence punch. They supply action.

The purpose of business communication is to promote decisive action. Well-chosen verbs in a business letter are the dynamos that generate the desired action. No matter what your position in business may be—executive, secretary, or teacher—verbs are the tools that will get things done for you. They are tools that you must use with facility and ease if you are to be a success in the business world.

Are you skilled in the use of these verb-tools? Can you, at this moment, state the precise difference between the proper use of the verbs **lie** and **lay**, or **sit** and **set**? The correct use of such verbs is governed by a relatively few simple rules. You can master these rules with a little application. You *must* master them if you are to be a success in the business office.

1. The Types of Verbs: Action and Linking

You probably remember from grammar school that a verb is a word that expresses *action*. However, do you remember that a verb may also be a word that merely *links* one part of the sentence to another but does not express action? Compare the two types of verbs below.

> *Action verbs:* **run, hit, fly, explode, lie, sleep, sit.**
> *Linking verbs:* **is, are, will be, seem, appear, taste, sound, look.**

Can you tell the difference between these types of verbs? You probably noticed that the action verbs depict an occurrence that you can easily picture in your imagination. On the other hand, the linking verbs refer to occurrences that are much more difficult to picture. Compare these two sentences:

> 1. The automobile <u>swerved</u> off the road.
> 2. It <u>seems</u> a good idea.

In your imagination you can probably picture the car **swerving**, but can you picture something **seeming**? Note that the linking verb **seems** can be replaced by the word **is**. This is true of all linking verbs. They do little more than stand in place of the word **is**.

> It seems a good idea.
>
> It is a good idea.

Many verbs may be either action verbs or linking verbs, depending upon how they are used in a sentence. Compare the use of the verb **taste** in the following sentences:

> 1. The gourmet tasted the soup with obvious delight.
> 2. Candy tastes sweet.

In the first sentence, **taste** is an action verb. It depicts the action of the gourmet in sampling the soup. You can almost picture him as he brings the spoon to his lips. However, in the second sentence, **taste** is a linking verb. It merely links the quality of sweetness to the subject **candy**. The word **is** could replace the word **tastes**.

> Candy tastes sweet.
>
> Candy is sweet.

Learn to recognize the distinction between action verbs and linking verbs, for you will have to apply it in later lessons. For the moment, remember these two points:

> 1. All forms of the verb **to be** are linking verbs. (Below is a list of all forms of the verb **to be**. You need not memorize this list. However, you should become familiar with these forms.)

is	is being	shall be	has been	shall have been
am	am being	will be	have been	will have been
are	are being	should be	had been	should have been
was	was being	would be		would have been
were	were being			

> 2. Verbs such as: **become, seem, appear, prove, grow, remain, feel, taste, sound, look,** and **smell** are linking verbs when they can be replaced by the word **is**.

> Candy tastes (is) sweet.
>
> Stone appears (is) solid

Velvet feels (is) soft.

Buttermilk smells (is) sour.

2. The Simple Tenses

Verbs change their form depending upon the time of the event they depict. We call the different forms a verb may take by the name *tenses*.

You undoubtedly know the three simple tenses: *the present tense, the past tense,* and *the future tense.* Certainly, in your daily conversation you have employed these tenses properly—perhaps without even realizing you were doing so. You would never say: **I will go to the store yesterday.** You realize, of course, that when you refer to an action which occurred **yesterday,** you must use the *past* tense with the verb **to go.** You would properly say: **I went** to the store yesterday.

Using the simple tenses is easy enough. We know that you have used these tenses correctly since you were an infant. Just as a review, here is an outline of the proper use of the three simple tenses:

1. The past tense refers to a definite past event or action.

> **I went to the movies yesterday.**
>
> **I sold the books last year.**

2. The future tense applies to events that will take place at a future time. You form the future tense by placing **will** or **shall** before the verb. At one time there were complicated rules governing whether **will** or **shall** was proper. Today, you can use **will** or **shall** interchangeably. One is as acceptable as the other.

> **I shall visit you in an hour.**
>
> **We will be there tomorrow.**
>
> **They will continue the service next week.**

3. The present tense is used to denote three types of actions.

> a. It describes action going on at the present time.
>
> **I am satisfied.**   **He is here.**
>
> b. It describes action that is continued or habitual.
>
> **I see him every day.**   **We sell hardware.**
>
> c. It is used to denote a general truth.

Cats are animals.   **Candy is sweet.**

As we have said, the simple tenses should cause you little trouble. There are two other forms of verbs that we are going to make easy for you—the progressive form and the perfect tenses.

3. The Progressive Form

The progressive form is used to refer to an *unfinished* action.

1. **I am working on the books right now.**

This means that you are at work on the books at present and have not finished them yet. Your work is unfinished.

2. **I was studying when John came in.**

This means that your studying was interrupted by John. You were not through studying. Your studying was unfinished.

In Sentences 1 and 2 each verb is in the progressive form because the action it denotes is still progressing—is *unfinished.* Did you notice that these verbs end in *ing?* The *ing* ending is the sign of the progressive form. In addition, did you notice that each progressive verb is preceded by a form of the verb **to be?** This, too, is essential to the progressive form.

1. **am working**
2. **was studying**

Learn these three things about the progressive form:

1. Use the progressive to show action that is or was unfinished.
2. Form the progressive verb by adding *ing* to the simple verb; and
3. Place a form of the verb **to be** before the progressive verb.

Occasionally, as a secretary, you will have to decide whether to use a simple tense or the progressive form. Here's an easy way to solve this problem. Merely ask yourself one question: *Is or was the action finished?* If finished, use the simple tense. If unfinished, use the progressive.

1. **I (walked, was walking) down the street yesterday when the wind blew my hat off.**

Ask: Was the action finished?

Answer: *No.* It was interrupted by the hat incident.

Therefore: Use the progressive form.

I was walking down the street when the wind blew my hat off.

2. He (writes) (is writing) out the report at this very moment.
Ask: Is the action finished?
Answer: *No.* He is still working on the report.
Therefore: Use the progressive form.

He is writing out the report at this very moment.

3. We (swam) (were swimming) at the lake every day last summer.
Ask: Was the action finished?
Answer: *Yes.* It was completed by the end of last summer.
Therefore: Use the simple tense.

We swam at the lake every day last summer.

4. They (worked) (were working) feverishly until dawn.
Ask: Was the action finished?
Answer: *Yes.* This is tricky. **Dawn** did not interrupt their work. It merely marked the moment when they stopped work.
Therefore: Use the simple tense.

They worked feverishly until dawn.

5. I (listened) (was listening) to the radio when the accident occurred.
Ask: Was the action completed?
Answer: *No.* It was interrupted by the accident.
Therefore: Use the progressive form.

I was listening to the radio when the accident occurred.

4. The Perfect Tenses

Let's turn to the perfect tenses now. We are going to show you how to make the proper use of the perfect tenses as easy as *a b c.*

They are called the *perfect* tenses because they always denote action that is *perfected*—that is, *completed.*

A. THE PAST PERFECT:

42

I had shipped the order by the time the message arrived.

This means that I had completed the shipment of the order before another event occurred. The other event was the arrival of the message. **Had shipped** is called the *past* perfect tense. It is *past* perfect because it denotes an action that was completed before another event, also in the *past*, occurred. Remember this: use the *past* perfect tense to show action that was completed before another event in the *past* occurred.

The sign of the past perfect is the word *had* before the verb.

> He *had left* by the time I arrived.
> They *had hidden* the prizes before the company sat down for dinner.
> It *had stopped* raining by noon.
> He *had finished* college before the war was over.

Occasionally, on the job, you will be faced with a choice of using either the simple past tense or the past perfect tense. Both refer to events completed in the past, but they are easily distinguished. Remember, the *past perfect* always refers to an action completed *before another event in the past.*

1. We (printed) (had printed) the edition before the censorship order arrived.

Ask: Did one event occur before another occurred?

Answer: *Yes*. The books were printed **before the order arrived.**

Therefore: Use the past perfect.

We **had printed** the edition before the censorship order arrived.

2. We (suspected) (had suspected) his statements even before **we received the police report.**

Ask: Does one event occur before another occurred?

Answer: *Yes*. We **had suspected** before we received the report.

Therefore: Use the past perfect.

We **had suspected** his statements even before we received **the police report.**

3. Spring (arrived) (had arrived) early last year.

Ask: Does one event occur before another occurred?

Answer: *No.* There is only one event—the arrival of spring.

Therefore: Use the simple past.

Spring arrived early last year.

4. Did he know that you (heard) (had heard) from the home office?

Ask: Does one event occur before another occurred?

Answer: *Yes.* You **had heard** before he **did know.** (Even though the sentence is in the form of a question, treat it as though it made an affirmative statement.)

Therefore: Use the past perfect tense.

Did he know that you had heard from the home office?

B. THE FUTURE PERFECT:

By this time tomorrow I shall have finished my exams.

This means that my exams will be completed by a definite moment in the *future.* As you probably guessed, **shall have finished** is in the *future* perfect tense.

Remember this: Use the *future* perfect tense to show action that will be completed by a definite time in the *future.* The sign of the future perfect is the words **shall have** or **will have** before the verb.

> By the time the message arrives, John *shall have left.*
> By June 30 our firm *shall have completed* its expansion plans.
> I *will have finished* my report by noon tomorrow.

Since the future perfect is not used too frequently in business material we won't bother you with any of the complications that it may cause. However, you should be able to cope with it when it does come up. So, right now, review again this little section on the future perfect.

C. THE PRESENT PERFECT:

John has filed only one report so far.

This means that John filed a report and will probably file more. The **so far** tells us there will probably be more reports. **Has filed** is called the *present perfect* tense. It is *present* perfect because it refers to an action that was completed in the past but is part of a series of actions that continues up to the *present*. The sign of the present perfect is the word **has** or **have** before the verb.

Let's look at some more examples to make this clearer.

1. He <u>has shopped</u> in our store many times.

Has shopped indicates that you expect him to shop some more at your store. If you didn't expect him back—let's suppose he had just moved to Pago-Pago —you would say:

He <u>shopped</u> in our store many times.

By using the simple past tense, **shopped,** you show that the action is completed once-and-for-all. It is not part of a continuing series.

2. John and Jane's bickering <u>has gone</u> on for years.

Has gone indicates that it is still going on. If the bickering had finally stopped —let's say that Jane divorced John and moved to Alaska—then you would say:

John and Jane's bickering <u>went</u> on for years.

3. The Smiths <u>have traveled</u> to this park year after year.

Do the Smiths intend to go back again? Certainly. **Have traveled** indicates they expect to continue to do so. If they didn't expect to return any more you would say:

The Smiths <u>traveled</u> to this park year after year.

Does the present perfect seem clearer to you now? Good. Let's see how you do with a few problems that we'll work through together.

1. **Mr. Jones (came) (has come) to see us on numerous occasions.**

Which is right, **came** or **has come?** The answer depends on what we mean. If Mr. Jones still comes to see us, then use **has come.**

Mr. Jones <u>has come</u> to see us on numerous occasions.

But, if Mr. Jones doesn't like us any more and doesn't visit us any more, use **came.**

Mr. Jones <u>came</u> to see us on many occasions.

2. **The boys (spoiled) (have spoiled) their little sister.**

45

If she is still being spoiled:

>**The boys have spoiled their little sister.**

If she is no longer being spoiled:

>**The boys spoiled their little sister.**

3. Our offices (were) (have been) on the same corner for years. If they still are on that corner, use **have been.**

>**Our offices have been on the same corner for years.**

If they have been moved elsewhere:

>**Our offices were on the same corner for years.**

5. Summary of Tenses

You have now studied all the tenses that you need know. Let's review the ground we have covered. In studying one tense at a time, you can easily lose track of the over-all picture. Does the following outline help you get a better view of all the tenses?

Tense	Refers to:	Example:
Simple past	A completed past action	arrived
Past perfect	A completed past action that came before another completed past action.	had arrived
Simple future	A future action	will shall } arrive
Future perfect	A future action that will be completed by a definite time in the future.	will shall } have arrived
Simple present	An action going on in the present	arrive
Present perfect	A completed action that is part of a continuing series of such actions.	has have } arrived

46

| Progressive Form | An action that is or was un-completed. | is
was } arriving |

6. Verb Forms

Look at how the verb **swim** changes depending upon its tense.

In the present tense you use **swim**.

I <u>swim</u> every day that I can.

In the past tense you use swam.

I <u>swam</u> every day last summer.

In the perfect tense you use have swum.

I <u>have swum</u> every day this summer.

These three forms—swim, swam, have swum—enable you to write all simple and perfect tenses of the verb swim. You already learned how.

1. **Swim** is the simple present tense.
   To form the simple future tense, place **shall** or **will** before swim.

   He <u>will swim</u> again next summer.
They <u>shall swim</u> in the race this afternoon.

2. **Swam** is the past tense.
   This is the only tense where **swam** is correct.

3. **Swum** is used in all the perfect tenses.
   a. **Has** or **have swum** is the present perfect.
      He <u>has swum</u> for hours.
   b. **Had swum** is the past perfect.
      He <u>had swum</u> for hours before he came out.
   c. **Will** or **shall have swum** is the future perfect.
      In an hour I <u>shall have swum</u> my race.

So, by knowing only three forms of the verb **swim**, you can form all simple and perfect tenses. This is true of all verbs. By knowing only *three* words you can write any simple or perfect tense.

Take another example—the verb, **drink.**

1. **Drink** { Present Tense   I drink milk.
Future Tense   I will drink my milk.

2. **Drank**   Past Tense   I drank all the milk.

3. **Drunk** { Present Perfect   I have drunk milk for years.
Past Perfect   I had drunk only milk till I was eighteen.
Future Perfect   I shall have drunk a full quart by the time I finish this glass.

Here is another example—the verb, **see.**

1. **See** { Present Tense   I see him.
Future Tense   I shall see him.

2. **Saw**   Past Tense   I saw him.

3. **Seen** { Present Perfect   I have seen him . . . .
Past Perfect   I had seen him . . . .
Future Perfect   I shall have seen him . . . .

Here is a final example—the verb, **go.**

1. **Go** { Present Tense   I go.
Future Tense   I will go.

2. **Went**   Past Tense   I went.

3. **Gone** { Present Perfect   I have gone . . . .
Past Perfect   I had gone . . . .
Future Perfect   I will have gone . . . .

To review, the above examples show that you can form any simple or perfect tense by knowing only three forms:

1. The present tense;
2. The past tense;
3. The perfect tense.

Now let us turn to choosing the proper forms of some other verbs.

7. Regular and Irregular Verbs

Most verbs are what we call *regular* verbs. By this we mean that they form the past tense by merely adding *d* or *ed* to the present tense, and they form the perfect tense by placing the word **has** or **have** before the past tense. For example, the following are some regular verbs:

PRESENT TENSE	PAST TENSE	PERFECT TENSE
receive	received	has or have received
like	liked	has or have liked
allow	allowed	has or have allowed
follow	followed	has or have followed

However, there are many so-called irregular verbs, which do not form their past and perfect tenses in this regular manner. You have already studied four irregular verbs—swim, **drink, see, go.**

Some books on English list a hundred or more irregular verbs and tell you, "Memorize these!" Such books are actually making the task more difficult than it need be. While irregular verbs do not follow the pattern of regular verbs, we can still find other patterns within them.

For example, it is obvious that there is similarity among:

drink	drank	has drunk
sink	sank	has sunk
shrink	shrank	has shrunk

To enable you to master irregular verbs in record time, we have divided them into families. When studying these families, read them *aloud.*

SAY:

sing	sang	has sung
ring	rang	has rung
spring	sprang	has sprung

By reading these word-groups aloud, your mind will *hear* the pattern within each family. You will learn *by ear*—the simplest, most indelible way. Remember, the key to saving yourself hours of work is to *say* the words in each family aloud and let your mind *hear the pattern.*

(Note: For the sake of brevity we have used **has** in the perfect tense. Remember, however, that **have** would be equally correct.)

SAY:

I. Present Tense	Past Tense	Perfect Tense
bring	brought	has brought
buy	bought	has bought
fight	fought	has fought
seek	sought	has sought
teach	taught	has taught

II. Present Tense	Past Tense	Perfect Tense
begin	began	has begun
swim	swam	has swum
ring	rang	has rung
sing	sang	has sung
spring	sprang	has sprung
sink	sank	has sunk
shrink	shrank	has shrunk
drink	drank	has drunk
run	ran	has run

III. Present Tense	Past Tense	Perfect Tense
blow	blew	has blown
grow	grew	has grown
know	knew	has known
throw	threw	has thrown
fly	flew	has flown
draw	drew	has drawn
withdraw	withdrew	has withdrawn
wear	wore	has worn
swear	swore	has sworn
tear	tore	has torn
show	*showed*	has shown

IV. Present Tense	Past Tense	Perfect Tense
bend	bent	has bent
lend	lent	has lent
spend	spent	has spent
deal	dealt	has dealt
feel	felt	has felt
keep	kept	has kept
sleep	slept	has slept
sweep	swept	has swept
weep	wept	has wept
mean	meant	has meant

Present Tense	Past Tense	Perfect Tense
leave	left	has left
lose	lost	has lost

V.

Present Tense	Past Tense	Perfect Tense
break	broke	has broken
choose	chose	has chosen
freeze	froze	has frozen
speak	spoke	has spoken
steal	stole	has stolen
forget	forgot	has forgotten

VI.

Present Tense	Past Tense	Perfect Tense
strive	strove	has striven
arise	arose	has arisen
take	took	has taken
mistake	mistook	has mistaken
shake	shook	has shaken
write	wrote	has written
typewrite	typewrote	has typewritten
underwrite	underwrote	has underwritten
eat	ate	has eaten
fall	fell	has fallen
forbid	forbade	has forbidden
give	gave	has given
hide	hid	has hidden

VII. The verbs in this group are irregular because they don't change at all. As you can see, they are the same in the present, past, and perfect tenses.

Present Tense	Past Tense	Perfect Tense
bid	bid	has bid
burst	burst	has burst
cost	cost	has cost
cut	cut	has cut
forecast	forecast	has forecast
hurt	hurt	has hurt
let	let	has let
read	read	has read
put	put	has put
quit	quit	has quit
spread	spread	has spread
thrust	thrust	has thrust

VIII. There is very little rhyme, and even less reason, in this group. Say the words aloud till they sound familiar.

Present Tense	Past Tense	Perfect Tense
come	came	has come
become	became	has become
bleed	bled	has bled
lead	led	has led
flee	fled	has fled
get	got	has got
meet	met	has met
bind	bound	has bound
stand	stood	has stood
win	won	has won
hold	held	has held
stick	stuck	has stuck
strike	struck	has struck
string	strung	has strung
have	had	has had
say	said	has said
make	made	has made
do	did	has done
go	went	has gone

8. Verbs and Objects of Verbs

You know that a sentence must contain a subject noun or pronoun and a predicate verb. However, you can combine a noun and a verb and still not have a meaningful sentence.

The secretary mailed . . . .

Though this expression contains a subject noun **secretary** and a predicate verb **mailed** it is incomplete by itself. It lacks an explanation of what was mailed. What is needed is an object of the verb **mailed**—a word that will tell us *what* was mailed.

The secretary mailed the invoice.

Invoice is the object of the verb **mailed** because it tells us *what* was mailed. To find the object of a verb you merely ask yourself *Whom?* or *What?* after the verb.

The secretary mailed . . . *What?* The invoice.

Invoice is the object of the verb **mailed**.

The President gave . . . *What?* A speech.

Speech is the object of the verb **gave**.

John loves . . . *Whom?* Mary.

Mary is the object of John's affections.

Of course, many verbs do not require objects to complete the meaning of a sentence. For example:

The President <u>speaks</u>.

Here the verb **speaks** is complete without an object.

The plaster <u>shook</u>.
The group <u>met</u>.

9. Lie and Lay—Sit and Set—Rise and Raise

To be a top secretary you should learn the difference between verbs that require objects and verbs that do not. Once you have done so, you can easily master the proper use of such tricky verbs as **lie** and **lay**, **sit** and **set**, **rise** and **raise**.

A. LIE AND LAY

Probably no two words in the English language are more frequently confused than **lie** and **lay**. Yet, **lie** and **lay** have entirely different meanings:

To **lie** means to **recline**.
To **lay** means to **place**.

An easy way to remember their different meanings is this little trick:

There is an **i** in both **lie** and **recline**. There is an **a** in both **lay** and **place**.
To **lie** means to recline.
To **lay** means to place.

As with all irregular verbs, the best way to learn the different tenses of **lie** and **lay** is to *say* them aloud.

53

SAY:

Present	Past	Perfect
lie	lay	has lain
lay	laid	has laid

Another trick: Note that there is an **n** in both recline and lain.

Here are some sentences using **lie.**

Present Tense: I **lie** on the grass.

Past Tense: I **lay** on the grass yesterday.

Perfect Tense: I **have lain** on the grass every afternoon this week.

Here are some sentences using **lay.**

Present Tense: I **lay** the book on the table.

Past Tense: I **laid** the book on the table yesterday.

Perfect Tense: I **have laid** the book on the table as you requested.

There is another trick that makes distinguishing between **lie** and **lay** easy. **To lie** *never* needs an object to complete its meaning. It is complete by itself. However, **to lay** *always* needs an object to complete its meaning. **Lay** must be followed by a word that tells us *what* was laid.

1. I **lay** the book on the table.
   Lay *what?* **The book.**
2. I **lie** on the grass.
   Lie *what?* No answer. **Lie** does not take an object.
3. I **laid** the carpeting yesterday.
   Laid *what?* **The carpeting.**
4. I **lay** in bed all day yesterday.
   Lay *what?* No answer. **Lay,** the past tense of **lie,** does not take an object.
5. They **have laid** their cards on the table.
   Have laid *what?* **Their cards.**
6. He **has lain** in a hospital bed for over a month.
   Has lain *what?* No answer. **Lain** does not take an object.

Let's try some problems using this method.

7. The workmen have (**laid, lain**) the linoleum in the kitchen.

   Have (laid, lain) *what?* **The linoleum.** Therefore, **laid** is correct since **laid** *always* takes an object.

   The workmen have. laid the linoleum in the kitchen.

8. The books have (**laid, lain**) on the shelves for years.

   Have (laid, lain) *what?* No answer. Therefore, use **lain**, since **lain** *never* takes an object.

   The books **have lain** on the shelves for years.

If you understand the difference between **lie** and **lay**, you will easily master the distinction between **sit** and **set** and between **rise** and **raise**. However, if you have any doubts about **lie** and **lay,** go back and restudy this lesson before you proceed further.

B. SIT AND SET

> **To sit** means **to be seated.**
> **To set** means **to place.**

Again, *say* the different tense forms aloud.

SAY:

Present	Past	Perfect
sit	sat	has sat
set	set	has set

EXAMPLES:

> The director **sits** at the head of the table.
> The director **sat** at the head yesterday.
> The director **has sat** at the head at every meeting.
> He **sets** *the book* on the desk.
> He **set** *the book* on the desk yesterday.
> He **has set** *the book* on the desk.

Again, **sit** *never* takes an object to complete its meaning. It is complete by itself. **Set** *always* needs an object to complete its meaning. It always re-

55

quires a word to tell us *what* was set.

Let's try a few problems:

1. He has (sat, set) the rules for the meeting.

   Has (sat, set) *what?* **The rules.** Therefore, use **set** since **set** *always* takes an object.

   He **has set** the rules for the meeting.

2. Grandpa used to (sit, set) in his chair by the hour.

   (Sit, set) *what?* No answer, Therefore; use **sit** since **sit** *never* takes an object.

   Grandpa used to **sit** in his chair by the hour.

C. RISE AND RAISE

> **To rise** means **to get up.**
> **To raise** means **to lift.**

Remember, *say* the different tense forms aloud.

SAY:

Present	Past	Perfect
rise	rose	has risen
raise	raised	has raised

EXAMPLES:

> I **rise** early every morning.
> I **rose** early yesterday.
> I **have risen** early every morning this week.
> We **raise** *the flag* each morning.
> We **raised** *the flag* at dawn this morning.
> We **have raised** *the flag* every morning this summer.

Once more, **rise** *never* takes an object to complete its meaning. It is complete by itself. **Raise** *always* needs an object to complete its meaning. It always requires a word to tell us *what* was raised.

1. He has (risen, raised) many questions.

   Has (risen, raised) *what?* **Many questions.** Therefore, use **raised** since **raised** *always* takes an object.

He **has raised** many questions.

2. The balloon (**rose, raised**) from the ground.

    (**Rose, raised**) *what?* No answer. Therefore, use **rose** since **rose** *never* takes an object.

    The balloon **rose** from the ground.

Now, here's a trick to tie all you have learned together. You have learned that all forms of the verbs **lie, sit,** and **rise** do not require objects to complete their meaning—that is, they can exist *independently.*

Just remember that independent has an **i,** and lie, sit, and rise also have **i**'s. Whenever there is no answer to the question *what* after the verb, you know that the verb is independent and that it must be a form of the verb:

lie, sit, or rise.

10. If I were . . .

There is one peculiarity of the verb **to be** which every good secretary should master. It is proper for you to say "I were" and "he were" in two instances:

a. To express a situation that you know to be contrary to fact:

   If I were king, I would free all men from servitude.

   If I were you, I would not talk so much.

   If Mr. Jones were here, your demands would be quickly met.

Remember, you use this form only if the situation is *known* to be false.

b. To express a wish:

   I wish I were king.

   I wish he were here now.

   We wish we were able to answer your question more fully.

   Would that I were king.

Exercise 12

Recognizing Action and Linking Verbs

A. This problem deals with recognizing the difference between action and linking verbs. Below is a list of verbs. In the space next to each verb mark **A** if it is an action verb; mark **L** if it is a linking verb; mark **E** if it could be either.

1. explode _____ A _____

2. spend _____

3. had been _____

4. sleep _____

5. lie _____

6. were _____

7. seem _____

8. walk _____

9. would have been _____

10. looks _____

11. was _____

12. recline _____

13. rested _____

14. mail _____

15. becoming _____

16. thinks _____

17. tastes _____

18. attack _____

19. receives _____

20. feels _____

B. This problem deals with distinguishing between action and linking verbs. Below is a list of sentences. Find the verb (predicate) of each sentence and write it in the space provided. In the other space provided, write **A** if the verb is an action verb; write **L** if the verb is a linking verb.

	Predicate Verb	Action or Linking
1. This booklet will show our entire line of clothing.	1. will show	A
2. We feel certain of your success.	2. _____	_____
3. Did you feel the texture of the cloth?	3. _____	_____
4. The meal tasted wonderful.	4. _____	_____
5. I tasted the soup.	5. _____	_____
6. This business becomes tedious after a few weeks.	6. _____	_____
7. The situation looks promising.	7. _____	_____
8. He will be there.	8. _____	_____
9. He looked me straight in the eye.	9. _____	_____
10. Lie down before dinner.	10. _____	_____
11. Mr. Smith looked for his papers.	11. _____	_____
12. The exam looked very easy to everyone.	12. _____	_____

Exercise 13

The Progressive Form

This problem deals with the proper use of the *progressive* form. In the space provided, write the proper verb for each of the following sentences. Remember, ask yourself: *Is or was the action completed?*

1. They (work) when the bell rang.   1. _____were working_____

2. Mr. Smith (see) Mr. Jones in his office, at this very minute.   2. _____

3. Last year we (sell) hundreds of desks.   3. _____

4. While we (talk) the manager arrived.   4. _____

5. Miss Johnson (type) the letter right now.   5. _____

6. We (send) all our customers the new price list last month.   6. _____

7. Weren't you (visit) the home office when the explosion occurred?   7. _____

8. We (know) you can do a perfect job.   8. _____

9. They (leave) when the order was delivered.   9. _____

10. We (file) all the invoices that had been received last week.   10. _____

Exercise 14

The Perfect Tenses

A. This problem deals with the proper use of the past perfect. In the space provided write the proper verb for each of the following sentences. Remember, ask yourself: *Did one event occur before another event, also in the past, occurred?*

1. The mail (arrive) before we opened the office.   1. _____had arrived_____

2. Our department (ship) the order before we received your wire.   2. _____

3. We (see) him walking in the street yesterday.   3. _____

4. Your officers (be) very courteous to us during the entire party yesterday.   4. _____

5. The inspector found that the crowd (be) dispersed before he arrived.   5. _____

6. We saw the puff of smoke right after we (hear) the explosion.   6. _____

7. As the bell rang, I (finish) my assignment.   7. _____

8. By the time the bell rang, I (finish) my assignment.   8. _____

9. My boss (dictate) five letters by noon.   9. _____

10. Napoleon (conquer) Italy before his thirtieth birthday.   10. _____

B. This problem deals with the proper use of the present perfect. In the space provided, write the proper verb for each of the following sentences. Remember, ask yourself: *Is this action part of a series of actions that continue up to the present?*

1. Ever since I entered the room, the clerk (do) nothing.

2. The baby (cry) since its mother left the room.

3. We (be) waiting here for the past hour.

4. We (go) to the office many times last week.

5. The present governor (be) in office for seven years.

6. Since you left this office there (be) very little activity.

7. Mr. Jones and Mr. Smith (be) friends since their college days together.

8. Jones and Smith (be) friends from their college days until death separated them.

9. I (ship) all orders on time so far this week.

10. Ever since Mr. Roberts became ill last week, he (have) to stay in bed.

1. _____has done_____

2. _____

3. _____

4. _____

5. _____

6. _____

7. _____

8. _____

9. _____

10. _____

Exercise 15
Irregular Verbs

This problem deals with irregular verbs. On each line is printed the present tense of an irregular verb. Write the past tense and the perfect tense of each of these verbs. Have you studied the irregular verbs carefully and recited them *aloud?*

Present Tense	*Past Tense*	*Perfect Tense*
1. I am	I _____was_____	I _____have been_____
2. You blow	You _____	You _____
3. It breaks	It _____	It _____
4. It bursts	It _____	It _____
5. They cost	They _____	They _____
6. You deal	You _____	You _____
7. We drive	We _____	We _____
8. I forbid	I _____	I _____
9. We fly	We _____	We _____
10. They go	They _____	They _____
11. I hide	I _____	I _____

Exercise 15 (continued)

Present Tense	Past Tense	Perfect Tense
12. She knows	She _____	She _____
13. I lead	I _____	I _____
14. You mistake	You _____	You _____
15. We pay	We _____	We _____
16. He reads	He _____	He _____
17. You seek	You _____	You _____
18. I shrink	I _____	I _____
19. We sing	We _____	We _____
20. You speak	You _____	You _____
21. I spend	I _____	I _____
22. They stand	They _____	They _____
23. We take	We _____	We _____
24. She teaches	She _____	She _____
25. We tear	We _____	We _____
26. You throw	You _____	You _____
27. I typewrite	I _____	I _____
28. He wears	He _____	He _____
29. I withdraw	I _____	I _____
30. You write	You _____	You _____

Exercise 16

Irregular Verbs II

This problem deals with the correct forms of irregular verbs. In the space provided, write the correct form of the indicated verb in each of the following sentences. Have you recited the irregular-verb *families* so often that you know these verbs by *ear?*

1. I (awake) at the crack of dawn yesterday.
2. By the time he arrived she had (become) very tired.
3. The general had (awake) by the time I called.
4. I (bid) $50 for the vase at yesterday's auction.
5. They were (bind) to each other by a common interest.
6. The tire had (blow) out.
7. Her heart had been (break) by the cad.

1. _____awoke_____
2. _____
3. _____
4. _____
5. _____
6. _____
7. _____

Exercise 16 (continued)

8. We will (build) a factory on the river.   8. _____

9. Yesterday the pipe (burst) with a roar.   9. _____

10. He was (choose) to accompany you.   10. _____

11. He has (come) a long way.   11. _____

12. By noon it had already (cost) me my entire salary.   12. _____

13. It was (cut) across the top.   13. _____

14. They were (deal) with in short order.   14. _____

15. He has (do) no wrong.   15. _____

16. This convention has (draw) a huge crowd.   16. _____

17. He had (drink) too much to be able to drive.   17. _____

18. We discovered that prices had (fall).   18. _____

19. Father (forbid) their leaving the house.   19. _____

20. Planes have (fly) millions of miles.   20. _____

21. The weather department has (forecast) clearing skies.   21. _____

22. By morning the water had (freeze).   22. _____

23. He has (get) too big for his breeches.   23. _____

24. The prize was (give) to the bookkeeper.   24. _____

25. All the members had (go) before the bell sounded.   25. _____

26. Our nation has (grow) to enormous power.   26. _____

27. He has not (hear) of your product.   27. _____

28. The invoice was (hide) under a pile of paper.   28. _____

29. He had (hurt) himself.   29. _____

30. Have you (keep) up with the news?   30. _____

31. Had I (know) of the detour, I would have chosen a different road.   31. _____

32. He has (lose) his opportunity.   32. _____

33. He has (lend) a fortune to the firm.   33. _____

34. He (mean) what he said.   34. _____

35. He had (meet) most of them before.   35. _____

36. I had (mistake) you for him.   36. _____

37. Your account was (overdraw)

37. _____

38. He has (prepay) the postage.

38. _____

39. Have you (read) the contract?

39. _____

40. We had (put) the matter before the board.

40. _____

41. Had he (quit) the race by the end of the first mile?

41. _____

42. The race had been (run) before noon.

42. _____

43. He had (see) many examples, but could follow none.

43. _____

44. They have (seek) the answer in vain.

44. _____

45. The building had (shake) under the force of the earthquake.

45. _____

46. Had he (show) you how to operate it?

46. _____

47. The profits (shrink) last week to half their former level.

47. _____

48. She has (sing) the song before royalty.

48. _____

49. The ship had (sink) to the bottom.

49. _____

50. I (sleep) until noon yesterday.

50. _____

Exercise 17

Objects of Verbs

A. This problem deals with the *objects* of verbs. Each of the following sentences contains a verb and its object. In the space provided rewrite the verb and the object of that verb. Remember, to find the object, just ask yourself: *Whom?* or *What?* after the verb.

	Verb	*Object of Verb*
1. John loves Mary.	1. loves	Mary
2. Father sent me to the store.	2. _____	_____
3. Our firm makes the finest clothing.	3. _____	_____
4. We appreciate your letter of September 20.	4. _____	_____
5. We hear the important events of the day on the radio.	5. _____	_____
6. We will send our representatives next week.	6. _____	_____
7. Will you mail your remittance by return post?	7. _____	_____
8. We are enclosing a copy of the new contract form.	8. _____	_____
9. We discussed the entire matter with him.	9. _____	_____

Exercise 17 (continued)

10. They advised him against the contract.   10. _____   _____

B. This problem deals with the proper use of *lie* and *lay*. In the space provided fill in the correct word. Remember: to *lay* means *to place*; to *lie* means *to recline*.

1. The book (lay, laid) on the shelf for months.   1. _____lay_____

2. (Lay, Lie) down before dinner.   2. _____

3. The President (lay, laid) down our basic foreign policy. 3. _____

4. It has (laid, lain) on a shelf for years.   4. _____

5. He will (lie, lay) the carpet tomorrow.   5. _____

6. Will you (lay, lie) down for a few moments' rest?   6. _____

7. He (lay, laid) the foundation for a solid business.   7. _____

8. They had (laid, lain) the goods on top of the table.   8. _____

9. The goods had (laid, lain) on the table for weeks.   9. _____

10. He had (laid, lain) his cards on the table and was ready to suffer

    the consequences.   10. _____

C. This problem deals with the proper use of *sit* and *set*. In the space provided fill in the correct word.

1. (Sit, Set) down in that chair.   1. _____sit_____

2. They have (sat, set) in their rocking chairs for years. 2. _____

3. (Set, Sit) the table down carefully.   3. _____

4. Can you (sit, set) by, doing nothing?   4. _____

5. (Sit, Set) the piano in the corner.   5. _____

6. Have you (sit, set) the rules for the contest?   6. _____

7. They were so tired they just (sat, set) right down on the ground. 7. _____

8. He has (set, sat) in the same spot for hours.   8. _____

9. (Sit, Set) the table in time for the guests.   9. _____

10. Have they (sat, set) long enough to be rested?   10. _____

D. This problem deals with the proper use of *rise* and *raise*. In the space provided fill in the correct word.

1. Can you (raise, rise) to the situation?   1. _____rise_____

2. Will you (raise, rise) your hand if you agree.   2. _____

3. We must try to (raise, rise) above such petty bickering.   3. _____

4. He would have (raised, rose) prices had he foreseen the inflation.   4. _____

5. Prices (raised, rose) due to the inflation.   5. _____

6. Prices had (raised, risen) not so fast as expected.   6. _____

7. The plane will (rise, raise) beyond the clouds in a few moments.   7. _____

8. (Rise, Raise) the curtains and we will see better.   8. _____

9. A number of rockets have (raised, risen) beyond the stratosphere.   9. _____

10. Will you (rise, raise) a fuss if they don't agree?   10. _____

Exercise 18

Was and Were

This problem deals with the proper use of *was* and *were*. In the space provided fill in the proper word.

1. If I (was, were) you, I would change my mind.   1. _____were_____

2. I wish I (was, were) President.   2. _____

3. He (was, were) not here yesterday.   3. _____

4. If he (was, were) to disappear into thin air, I could not be more pleased.   4. _____

5. I don't know if he (was, were) at the meeting.   5. _____

6. (Was, Were) I you, I would do the same.   6. _____

7. If I (was, were) the manager of this firm I would do things differently.   7. _____

8. Since the report turned out to be false I (was, were) very relieved.   8. _____

9. Here is how I would act if I (was, were) in your shoes.   9. _____

10. I certainly wish it (was, were) cooler.   10. _____

Review Exercise

Verbs

This problem deals with the proper use of verbs. In the following letter many verbs are in italics. If the italicized verb is *correct*, place a C above it. If the verb is *incorrect*, cross it out and write the correct form above it. Pay particular attention to the use of proper tenses and to irregular verbs.

Dear Mr. Robinson:

I *was* very disappointed that you ~~have~~ *did* not send any representative to *watch* the test of our new Starfire car model last week. We are positive that he would *be* astounded by the way the Starfire *performed,* as *was* the hundreds of others who *was* there. Did he *forgot* the date of this demonstration test?

If he had *attended* he would *be seeing* a new concept in automotive design and engineering. The Starfire *was* an all-new car. It *had* a new engine, new streamlining, new controls.

Until the new line of Starfires *were unveiled* last week, the automobile industry *has* been lagging behind other industries in the use of plastics. The Starfire *has* changed this.

At last week's demonstration tests the Starfire *accelerated* to 90 miles per hour in under twenty-five seconds.

I needn't tell you how *astonished* the representatives of other firms *were* when they *seen* this spectacular performance. I'm sure that many of them *had* already told you about it themselves.

Until you have *seen* the Starfire and *drove* in it, you will be missing the thrill of your life. If I *was* you I would make arrangements to *attendance* the next demonstration which will be *holded* next Thursday at 4 o'clock at the Grand Plaza Arena. We *know* that by six o'clock next Thursday you *are* convinced that your going to the demonstration *were* one of the wisest moves of your life.

Moreover, Mr. Robinson, I am pleased to *information* you that your firm *have* been chosen to enjoy a particular distinction at next week's demonstration. I am *forbid* to disclose anything further, but I can *forecast* with certainty that you will be *freezed* with surprise.

You have *know* our firm for many years, Mr. Robinson. You have *seed* us become the leader in our field. You know that during the past three years we have *spended* many millions of dollars to *built* the Starfire, and that we will *spend* many millions more to improve it. We have *stroved* to *shaken* off the shackles of conservative thinking that have *hold* the automotive industry back for years. We have *undertook* a difficult task these past three years. While others were *setting* in their easy chairs, or *laying* around relaxing, our research men were *stroving* to perfection.

The Starfire has been *brung* into being by this devotion to a concept. It has *sprang* into being out of the minds and energy of America's top automotive engineers. In the same way that the jet plane *shrunk* the highways of the air, so shall the Starfire *shrink* the highways on land.

We feel that with the Starfire we have *laid* the ground work for all new automobiles. We have *setted* new standards in the field of transportation.

                                        Sincerely,

66

ADJECTIVES

An old Chinese proverb says, "A picture is worth ten thousand words." In writing sentences, you paint pictures with adjectives. An adjective is a word that describes a noun or pronoun. Adjectives give color to an otherwise drab subject.

Compare these two classified advertisements. Which woman will win the job?

1. Woman, college education, looking for job as secretary in theatrical field.

2. Attractive, energetic young woman, with college education and experience, desires challenging position as secretary to overburdened executive in theatrical field.

By using adjectives in a colorful, forceful manner, Woman No. 2 has created a positive image of herself in the prospective employer's mind. Remember this example when you apply for your job upon completion of this course. You must paint a positive, colorful portrait of yourself by skillful use of adjectives.

1. Comparison of Adjectives

The *simple* form of an adjective describes a *single* item, or a single group of items.

> fine book, pretty girl, fast cars, long letters

However, adjectives have an added power. They give you the ability to compare one item with others. If you are comparing *two* things, you add **er** to most *simple* adjectives to form what we call the *comparative* form.

> This is a finer book than that one.
> Jane is prettier than Mary.
> Sport cars are faster than stock cars.
> These letters are longer than those.

Remember: Use the comparative form only when comparing *two* items.

When you compare *three or more* items, add **est** to the simple adjective. We call this form the *superlative.*

This is the finest book I ever read.
Jane is the prettiest of the three girls.
This is the fastest sport car in the world.
This is the longest letter we have received.

Is the difference between the comparative and the superlative clear in your mind? To repeat: You use the *comparative* form only when comparing *two* items. You use the *superlative* when comparing *three or more.*

Why is the following sentence incorrect?

WRONG: He is the **taller** of the three boys.

If the answer is not obvious to you, you must review this entire lesson.

However, not all adjectives form their comparatives and superlatives by adding **er** and **est.** It would be very awkward for a suitor to have to say to his best girl:

"You are the beautifulest girl in the world."

Long adjectives, such as **beautiful,** would become tongue-twisters if we were to add **er** or **est.** So, instead of adding **er** or **est** to the end of such an adjective, we place the word **more** or **most** in front of it. To form the comparative of long adjectives we say:

more beautiful   more grateful   more difficult   more durable

To form the superlative we say:

most beautiful   most grateful   most difficult   most durable

Note, however, that the rule about comparatives and superlatives still applies.

More beautiful, compares only *two.*
Most beautiful, compares *three or more.*

By now you are probably wondering: How do I know when to add **er** or **est,** and when to prefix the adjective with **more** or **most?** The best we can offer you is a rule-of-thumb. To most adjectives of *one* syllable add **er** or **est**. To most adjectives of more than two syllables add **more** or **most**.

Study the list of adjectives below. Note particularly the spelling of the different forms of these adjectives.

Simple	Comparative	Superlative
short	shorter	shortest
long	longer	longest
sad	sadder	saddest
happy	happier	happiest
lovely	lovelier	loveliest .
lazy	lazier	laziest
dry	drier	driest
attractive	more attractive	most attractive
difficult	more difficult	most difficult

A few adjectives form their comparatives and superlatives in a different manner. Don't let that worry you. Not only are there very few of these irregular adjectives, but you are familiar with most of them already.

Simple	Comparative	Superlative
bad	worse	worst
good	better	best
little	less	least
many } much	more	most
late	{ later { latter	latest last
far	{ farther { further	farthest furthest

2. Using Adjectives

A. COMPARISON WITH A GROUP

What is wrong with this sentence?

WRONG: **I am smarter than any person in my class.**

I am in my class. I cannot be smarter than myself. Therefore, I must exclude myself from the rest of the group by the use of the word **other** or the word **else**, as follows:

Right: I am smarter than any <u>other</u> person in my class.
Right: I am smarter than anyone <u>else</u> in my class.

Do you see the point? It is subtle, but logical.

B. THIS AND THAT

These is the plural of **this**. **Those** is the plural of **that**.

This book is perfect.
These books are perfect.
That mountain is farther than it looks.
Those mountains are farther than they look.

You may have trouble with these words where the noun that is modified sounds plural but is really singular—nouns such as **kind, sort,** and **type.** Be sure to write **this kind** or **that kind**—NOT, *these kind* or *those kind.* However, you should use **those kinds** or **these kinds,** since **kinds** is plural.

C. LESS AND FEWER

Less should be used to refer to items measured in bulk.
Fewer should be used to refer to items counted separately.

<u>Less</u> coal was mined this year.
<u>Fewer</u> men applied for the job than was anticipated.

D. FIRST AND LAST

When using the word **first** or the word **last** to modify a number, always place it directly before the number.

The <u>first eight</u> pages have been typed.
(NOT: The eight first pages.)
The <u>last six</u> people arrived late.
(NOT: The six last people arrived late.)

E. THEM

The word **them** is a pronoun not an adjective. NEVER use **them** to modify a noun or another pronoun.

70

Right: **Those** books are mine. (NOT: **Them** books are mine.)

Right: **That** kind is no good. (NOT: **Them** kind is no good.)

In Lesson 8 you will learn when to use **them.** For the present learn when *not* to use it.

F. One Another and Each Other

Do you know what's wrong with this sentence?

WRONG: **The two men knew one another.**

One another always refers to *three or more* persons or things. In our sentence there are only *two* men. So we must use **each other,** which is the proper form when there are only *two* persons or things.

Right: **The two men knew each other.**

Right: **The three men knew one another.**

G. Placement of the Word Only

The three sentences below show how we can completely change our meaning by merely moving the word *only.*

Only Bob was accused of lying.

This means that no one else was accused.

Bob was only accused of lying.

This means that he was accused but not convicted.

Bob was accused of lying only.

He was not accused of anything else.

From these sentences above, learn this rule of good English: Always place the word **only** as close as possible to the word it modifies.

Right: I paid **only** eight dollars.

WRONG: I only paid eight dollars.

Right: I filed my application **only** a day late.

WRONG: I only filed my application a day late.

H. Misrelated Expressions

You just learned that you should place the word **only** as close as possible to the word it modifies. In the same manner, you should always place an expression that modifies a word as close to that word as possible. Failure to do so can result in strange sentences.

Look at these examples:

Right: They delivered the piano with mahogany legs to the woman.
WRONG: They delivered the piano to the woman with mahogany legs.
Right: He took out his handkerchief, blew his nose, and put his handkerchief back into his pocket.
WRONG: He took out his handkerchief, blew his nose, and put it back into his pocket.
Right: Walking down Broadway, he looked at the Woolworth Building.
WRONG: He looked at the Woolworth Building, walking down Broadway.

3. Articles

There are three words that we call *articles*—a, an, the. You've used these words all your life so you should have little trouble with them.

Whether to use **a** or **an** depends upon the sound of the next word. When the next word begins with a *consonant* sound, you use **a**. A consonant sound is the sound of any letter in the alphabet except **a, e, i, o, u.**

a boy   a happy boy
a man   a young man

Note that you say: **a** happy boy. On the other hand you say: **an** honest man. Why? Because in the word **honest**, the h is silent. Since the word **honest** does not begin with a consonant *sound*, use **an**.

an hour   a house
an honor   a hotel

You use **an** wherever a word begins with a *vowel* sound. The vowels are **a, e, i, o, u.**

an apple   an incident
an event   an orange
an umbrella

Note that while you should say, **an umbrella,** you also should say, **a university.** Why? Because the u in **university** sounds like the y in **you.** Remember, it is the *sound* that counts, not the spelling.

a union	an ulcer
a usurer	an undertaking

4. Repeating the Article

Occasionally, as a secretary, you will be faced with a problem of whether to repeat the article. For example:

The red and (the) white coats are on sale.

Should you use the extra **the?** This depends upon what you mean. If each coat is part white and part red then *omit* the extra **the.**

The red and white coats are on sale.

However, if there are two types of coats, one all white and the other all red then *add* the extra **the.**

The red and the white coats are on sale.

Do you see this subtle distinction?

The President and the Chairman arrived. (Two men.)
The President and Chairman arrived. (One man holding both positions.)
The steel and the plastic cabinets are in place. (Some cabinets all steel; some, all plastic.)
The steel and plastic cabinets are in place. (Cabinets of part steel and part plastic.)

Exercise 19
Recognizing Adjectives

This problem deals with recognizing adjectives. Underline the adjective in each of the following sentences with one line. Then, underline the word each adjective modifies with two lines.

1. He picked up the heavy case.

2. She prepared a light supper.

3. The colored lights were dimmed.

4. It was a very efficient system.

5. We have complete records.

6. Our latest records show a deficit.

7. We sent an order for farm machinery.

8. He slowly walked to his first class.

9. These are first-class goods.

10. Here is our new catalogue.

11. Send me your final approval.

12. Where is my brown hat?

13. Forgive my late reply.

14. The table has a smooth finish.

15. We went horseback riding.

16. It's a very smooth-riding car.

17. This is an easy problem.

18. This problem is easy.

19. I am hungry.

20. He feels hungry.

Exercise 20

Degrees of Adjectives

A. This problem deals with the three forms an adjective may take—simple, comparative, and superlative. On each line of the following table is written one of the three adjective forms. Fill in the other two forms. Pay special attention to proper spelling. Nothing less than perfect spelling is acceptable.

	Simple	*Comparative*	*Superlative*
1.	pretty	prettier	prettiest
2.		busier	
3.	familiar		
4.			most
5.		less	
6.			last
7.		hotter	
8.	good		
9.			farthest
10.		less	
11.	difficult		
12.		worse	
13.	unusual		
14.			loveliest
15.	friendly		

B. This problem deals with the choice of the comparative or the superlative adjective. In the space provided write the proper form of the adjective in parentheses. Remember, use the *comparative* when comparing *two;* use the *superlative* when comparing *three or more.*

1. Although Mr. Smith and Mr. Jones are bright, Mr. Roberts is the (wise).

1. _____wisest_____

2. Which of this pair has the (bright) colors?

2. _____

3. Though our Raleign plant is large, the Durham plant is (large).

3. _____

4. New York is the (exciting) of the two cities.

4. _____

5. New York is the (exciting) city in the world.

5. _____

6. She is the (tall) girl in the whole office.

6. _____

7. The left sleeve is (long) than the right.

7. _____

8. Of all our forty-three offices, the (large) is in Los Angeles.

8. _____

9. Test this one, then that one, and choose the (good).

9. _____

10. Which of the twins is the (pretty)?

10. _____

Exercise 21

Using Adjectives

This problem deals with the proper use of *less* and *fewer.* In the space provided write the correct word, either *less* or *fewer.* Remember, use *less* to refer to quantities measured in bulk; use *fewer* to refer to items counted separately.

1. They delivered (less) (fewer) coal than we had ordered.

1. _____less_____

2. They delivered (less) (fewer) tons of coal than we had ordered.

2. _____

3. There were (less) (fewer) than ten customers today.

3. _____

4. We can do the same amount of work with (less) (fewer) secretaries.

4. _____

5. Your firm has sent (less) (fewer) orders than anticipated.

5. _____

6. There is (less) (fewer) unemployment than anticipated.

6. _____

7. This air-conditioner uses (less) (fewer) electricity than any other model.

7. _____

8. This air-conditioner uses (less) (fewer) kilowatts of electricity than any other model.

8. _____

Exercise 22

Using Adjectives II

A. This problem deals with the proper use of *each other* and *one another*. In the space provided write the correct expression. Remember, *each other* refers to two; *one another* refers to three or more.

1. The two men spoke to (each other) (one another).

1. _____each other_____

2. The committee members spoke to (each other) (one another) until it was time to convene.

2. _____

3. We are acquainted with (each other) (one another), he and I.

3. _____

4. The men in the mob prodded (each other) (one another) to greater violence.

4. _____

5. The two airmen helped (each other) (one another) survive in the jungle.

5. _____

B. This problem deals with placement of the word *only*. In each of the following sentences *only* is improperly placed. Rewrite each of these sentences in the space provided, placing the word *only* more properly. Remember, *only* should be placed directly before the word it modifies.

1. The President only signed the first bill.

The President signed only the first bill.

_____

2. He only saw three familiar faces.

_____

_____

3. I only met him twice.

_____

_____

4. We filed our applications one day late only.

_____

_____

5. This hat only cost three dollars.

_____

_____

C. This problem deals with the proper placement of modifiers. Each of the sentences below is incorrect because of a misplaced modifier. Rewrite these sentences correctly in the space provided. Remember, *place the modifier as close as possible to the word it modifies.*

1. People cannot fail to notice vast changes in business methods who are in touch with business offices.

   People who are in touch with business offices cannot fail to notice vast changes in business methods.

2. We saw the new building walking down East Shore Drive.

3. The soldier saddled his horse who was wearing a new uniform.

4. Take the book to the man with beautiful leather binding.

5. The dog ran toward his master wagging his tail.

6. Take the table to the shop with its four legs to be mended.

7. He watched the parade pass by standing at the corner.

8. The men took the chair to the woman with all four legs painted black.

Exercise 23

Using Articles

A. This problem deals with choosing *a* or *an*. In the spaces provided write either *a* or *an*, whichever is correct.

1. __A__ man wearing __an__ unusual jacket left __a__ package.

2. _____ humorist is _____ human being with _____ fine sense of humor.

3. _____ understanding of all operations in our plant is _____ necessity for _____ foreman.

4. _____ hour before dawn is _____ inhuman hour for _____ human being to be awakened.

5. _____ union leader should be _____ honest man, for to lead _____ union is _____ undertaking of great responsibility.

B. This problem deals with repeating the article. In the space provided rewrite each sentence correctly.

1. The secretary and vice-president met at noon.

   The secretary and the vice-president met at noon.

2. He was elected to be both the vice-president and the secretary.

3. The car has a blue and a white finish.

4. We have in stock two cabinets, a chromium and aluminum one.

5. She wore a red and a green sweater.

Review Exercise

Adjectives

The letter below includes many intentional errors. Rewrite the letter, correcting all such errors.

Dear Mr. White:

Have you heard about our sale on phonograph records? This sale is excitinger and spectacularer than any sale in this city's history.

Only during the two first weeks we have sold no less than 10,000 records in each of our two stores. You might be interested to know that the South Street store has sold the greatest number of records even though the store is farthest from the heart of town. This is a extremely unusual development.

We would be very grateful if you would visit our store. You can't miss it, walking down Sixth Avenue toward Elm. Mr. Johnson, our manager, and his assistant, Mr. Roberts, are very anxious to see you. I'm sure you three will enjoy chatting with each other.

Perhaps you will explain to these men why they have least sales than the South Street store. We want you to give them a honest opinion. See if you can help them catch up and surpass the South Street store during the three last weeks of the sale.

Lesson 6

ADVERBS

You know what words we use to give color to nouns or pronouns. That's right, *adjectives!* Now let's discuss those words which we use to give color to verbs —words we call *adverbs*. Adverbs are jacks-of-all-trades. Not only do they modify verbs, they also can modify adjectives, or they can modify other adverbs.

The ship sailed <u>swiftly</u>.

The adverb **swiftly** modifies the verb **sailed.**

Broadway is an <u>extremely</u> wide street.

The adverb **extremely** modifies the adjective **wide.**

The old man walked <u>very</u> slowly.

The adverb **very** modifies the adverb **slowly.**

An *adverb* is a word that tells you: *how, when, where,* or *how much.*

The book was printed carefully. Printed *how?* Carefully.
The order was shipped promptly. Shipped *when?* Promptly.
The officials came here. Came *where?* Here.
They were very pleased. Pleased *how much?* Very.

1. Forming Adverbs

You form most adverbs by adding **ly** to the whole adjective.

Adjective	Adverb
swift	swiftly
careful	carefully
familiar	familiarly
strict	strictly
like	likely
sincere	sincerely
sole	solely ·
definite	definitely
confidential	confidentially
equal	equally

When the adjective ends in y, to form the adverb change the y to i and add ly.

Adjective	Adverb
busy	busily
happy	happily
satisfactory	satisfactorily
temporary	temporarily

When the adjective ends in **able** or in **ible,** to form the adverb drop the final e and add y.

Adjective	Adverb
noticeable	noticeably
considerable	considerably
forcible	forcibly
horrible	horribly

Note the change in spelling when we transform these adjectives into adverbs.

Adjective	Adverb
due	duly
true	truly
whole	wholly

2. Choosing Between Adverbs and Adjectives

As a secretary, you will have to choose between using an adjective or an adverb in many sentences. Will you know which to use?

For example:

The situation looks (bad) (badly).

Which is correct? By the time you finish this lesson, you will know how to solve such problems easily.

You learned in the chapter on verbs that there are two types of verbs—*action* verbs and *linking* verbs. If you don't know the distinction between them right now—and know it well—do not read further in this lesson. The whole problem of when to use adverbs and when to use adjectives hinges on the distinction between action and linking verbs. STOP! Review Chapter 4 right now if this distinction is not crystal-clear in your mind.

The rule is very simple:

Use an *adverb* to modify an *action* verb.

Use an *adjective* after a *linking* verb.

The fire burned fiercely.

Burned is an *action* verb. Therefore, we used the *adverb*, **fiercely.**

The material was sent promptly.

Sent is an *action* verb. Therefore, we use the *adverb*, **promptly.**

The leader threatened angrily.

Threatened is an *action* verb. Therefore, we use the *adverb*, **angrily.**

BUT:

The tiger looked fierce.

Looked, as used here, is a *linking* verb. Therefore, we use the *adjective* **fierce.**

The delivery was prompt.

Was, is a *linking* verb. Therefore, we use the *adjective*, **prompt.**

He seemed angry.

Seemed, is a *linking* verb. Therefore, we use the *adjective*, **angry.**

Earlier in this lesson, we gave as an example the problem-sentence:

The situation looks (bad) (badly).

You should be able to solve this easily, now. **Looks,** as used here, is a *linking* verb. Therefore, we use the adjective **bad.**

The situation looks <u>bad</u>.

Here's a final problem:

The secretaries work (quick, quickly).

(Is the verb, **work,** an action or a linking verb? Right! It is an *action* verb. Therefore, use the *adverb*, **quickly.**

The secretaries work <u>quickly</u>.

3. Using Adverbs

A. GOOD AND WELL

Dinner tasted (good) (well).   81

Good is an adjective. **Well** is an adverb. Since **tasted** is a *linking* verb, **we** use the *adjective,* **good. Dinner tasted good.**

He performed (good) (well).

Performed is an *action* verb. Therefore, we use the adverb, **well. He performed well.**

The only exception to this rule occurs when **well** is used to mean, **in good health.** In such case, **well** is an *adjective* and can be used after a *linking* verb.

He is well.   He feels well.   He looks well.

BUT remember:

The flower smells <u>good</u>.

B.   MOST AND ALMOST

(Most, Almost) all the orders were sent.

A simple test to determine whether to use **most** or **almost** is to substitute the word **nearly.** If **nearly** fits then you know that **almost** is proper.

<u>Nearly</u> all the orders were sent.

Therefore:

<u>Almost</u> all the orders were sent.

In the following sentence it is obvious that **nearly** would not fit, so **most** is proper.

Who had the <u>most</u> errors?

BUT:

It was <u>almost</u> too late to catch the train.

The same as: **It was <u>nearly</u> too late . . . .**

C.   DOUBLE NEGATIVES

Time and again you have heard people say that two negatives make a positive. For our purposes, two negatives make a poor secretary. You must avoid double negatives.

What is a double negative? Here is a common example:

WRONG: They don't know nothing.

This sentence contains two negative words, **don't** and **nothing**. Each of these negatives destroys the other. By eliminating either one of them we get a correct sentence.

> Right: **They know nothing.**
> Right: **They don't know anything.**

Remember: Avoid double negatives.

> 1. Right: He didn't say anything.
>   Right: He said nothing.
>   WRONG: He didn't say nothing.
> 2. Right: It was nothing.
>   Right: It wasn't anything.
>   WRONG: It wasn't nothing.

You may have a little more difficulty with words which don't look negative but really are; words such as: **scarcely, hardly, never, neither, but.** They will cause you no trouble if you remember that these words are negative in themselves. Never add the word **not** to them.

1. We can <u>scarcely</u> see you in this fog. (NOT: We can't scarcely see you . . .)
2. We could <u>hardly</u> have decided otherwise. (NOT: We couldn't hardly . . .)
3. It could <u>never</u> happen here. (NOT: It couldn't never happen here.)
4. It was <u>neither</u> of them. (NOT: It wasn't neither of them.)
5. I understand all <u>but</u> one of them. (NOT: I don't understand all but one . . .)

D. REAL AND VERY

> I am (real) (very) pleased.

Real is an adjective that means **genuine. Very** is an adverb that means **extremely.** When faced with a choice of **real** or **very** substitute **genuine or extremely.** If **genuine** fits, **real** is correct. If **extremely** fits, **very** is correct.

Our problem-sentence reads properly if we insert **extremely:**

> I am extremely pleased.

Therefore, use **very:**

I am very pleased. (NOT: I am real pleased.)

Right: It gives me <u>real</u> (genuine) pleasure to introduce the next speaker.

Right: We are <u>very</u> (extremely) well pleased with the outcome.

Right: It was a <u>real</u> (genuine) diamond.

Right: It was a <u>very</u> (extremely) wonderful movie.

Exercise 24

Adverbs

A. This problem deals with recognizing adverbs. Underline the adverb in each of the following sentences with one line. Then, underline the word it modifies with two lines.

1. The plane <u><u>traveled</u></u> <u>swiftly</u>.

2. We are very much pleased to hear from you.

3. We walked quietly to the side.

4. Quickly he leaped into his car.

5. The matter is entirely finished.

6. No two men are completely alike.

7. This occurrence is most unfortunate.

8. We strongly urge you to accept this offer.

9. Recheck thoroughly all outgoing mail.

10. They came here much later than expected.

11. He was essentially interested in securing a patent.

12. We were unusually surprised by his work.

13. All our customers are comfortably dressed when they leave us.

14. Watch this maneuver intently.

15. Mr. Jones arrived at the meeting exactly at the appointed hour.

B. This problem deals with changing adjectives into adverbs. Below is a list of adjectives. In the space next to each adjective, write the equivalent adverb.

1. careful	carefully	7. whole	_____
2. sole	_____	8. true	_____
3. busy	_____	9. considerable	_____
4. primary	_____	10. substantial	_____
5. noticeable	_____	11. real	_____
6. principal	_____	12. extraordinary	_____

13. extreme _____   15. good _____

14. bad _____   16. beautiful _____

Exercise 25

Review of Action and Linking Verbs

This is a review problem involving action and linking verbs. Underline the verb in each of the following sentences. Then, in the space provided, mark A if it is used as an action verb; mark L if it is used as a linking verb. Have you reviewed Lesson 4 on the distinction between action and linking verbs?

1. He <u>looked</u> at me with a piercing stare.   1. ___A___

2. The office seems quite comfortable.   2. _____

3. This bread smells very fresh.   3. _____

4. John lay down on his bed after dinner.   4. _____

5. This proposition is a once-in-a-lifetime opportunity.   5. _____

6. Mr. Jones looks taller than his brother.   6. _____

7. This situation seems positively uncanny.   7. _____

8. John rests.   8. _____

9. By tomorrow I shall have been there and back.   9. _____

10. He knows the answer to our problems.   10. _____

Exercise 26

Choosing Between Adverbs and Adjectives

This problem deals with choosing between an adjective and an adverb. Below is a series of sentences. In the space provided write the proper form of the word in parentheses in each sentence. Remember, *use an adverb to modify an action verb; use an adjective after a linking verb.*

1. Candy tastes (sweet).   1. ___sweet___

2. He tasted the mixture (careful).   2. _____

3. Return the merchandise as (quick) as possible.   3. _____

4. He is very (content).   4. _____

5. The situation seems (bad).   5. _____

6. I am (extreme) tired from my long journey.   6. _____

7. The plant grew more and more (quick).   7. _____

8. The whole garden smells (sweet).   8. _____

9. We (certain) hope you are comfortable.   9. _____

10. We feel he has been (extraordinary) competent at his task.   10. _____

Exercise 26 (continued)

11. Ordinarily the bell tolls (soft), but today it sounds (loud).

11. _____

_____

12. Our situation has grown (bad).

12. _____

13. She looks (beautiful).

13. _____

14. We can accomplish our goals (easy).

14. _____

15. He has done (good, well) in his new post.

15. _____

16. Our product is becoming more and more (desirable) in its line.

16. _____

17. Mr. Jones became (angry) and threatened his employee (loud).

17. _____

_____

18. He feels (indignant) because he cannot attend.

18. _____

19. The whole story sounds (strange).

19. _____

20. You are paying an (extreme) large amount.

20. _____

21. We will (glad) repay your losses.

21. _____

22. This is a very (poor) constructed problem.

22. _____

23. The river flowed (rapid).

23. _____

24. Do business conditions look (bad) to you?

24. _____

Exercise 27

Using Adverbs

A. This problem deals with the proper use of *good* **and** *well***. In the space provided write the proper word—either** *good* **or** *well***.**

1. You did the job very (good, well).

1. _____well_____

2. You did a very (good, well) job.

2. _____

3. It sounds (good, well) to me.

3. _____

4. You look (good, well) in your new suit.

4. _____

5. He performs (good, well) on the piano.

5. _____

6. The job was done quite (good, well).

6. _____

7. The proposition sounds (good, well).

7. _____

8. We feel confident you shall do (good, well) in your new position.

8. _____

9. Though he was sick, he is now completely (good, well).

9. _____

10. He was extremely (good, well) in the part of Hamlet.

10. _____

B. This problem deals with the proper use of *most* and *almost*. In the space provided write the proper word. Remember, use *almost* only where the word *nearly* could be used as well.

1. These are (most, almost) all of the supplies that are left.   1. _____almost_____
2. We found that (most, almost) people did not answer.   2. _____
3. He is (most, almost) as good as his competitor.   3. _____
4. (Most, Almost) everything was finished by noon.   4. _____
5. (Most, Almost) of the time we work quite hard.   5. _____
6. It was (most, almost) too good to be true.   6. _____
7. We feel that (most, almost) of our staff is doing a top-notch job.   7. _____
8. It seems that (most, almost) all of the men answered our plea.   8. _____
9. He can sell (most, almost) as (good, well) as any of our other salesmen.   9. _____ _____
10. (Most, Almost) anyone who dresses (well, good) can look (well, good).   10. _____ _____ _____

C. This problem deals with double negatives. Rewrite the following letter, correcting all double-negative expressions.

Dear Mr. Bronson,

Mr. Marshall, from your office, hasn't scarcely visited us more than a few times in the past few months. We certainly hope that we haven't done nothing to offend him. After all, we haven't hardly started in our association with your firm and we certainly wouldn't want to do nothing that would jeopardize our fine relationship.

Sincerely,

D. This problem deals with the proper use of *real* and *really*. In the space provided write the proper word.

1. These diamonds are (real, really).   1. _____real_____
2. He was (real, really) pleased to meet them.   2. _____
3. It gives us (real, really) satisfaction.   3. _____
4. We are (real, really) sorry we cannot comply.   4. _____
5. After a day's work he was (real, really) tired.   5. _____
6. Were the (real, really) situation known there might be a scandal.   6. _____
7. The teachers were (real, really) concerned about her grades.   7. _____
8. This matter is (real, really) important.   8. _____

Lesson 7

PREPOSITIONS

There is no simple definition for the preposition. All we can do is make the general statement that a preposition connects a noun or pronoun with the body of the sentence. Words such as the following are prepositions: **of, at, in, on, between.**

The noun or pronoun that the preposition connects to the body of the sentence is called the *object* of that preposition.

> **of John**—John is the *object* of the preposition **of.**
> **at the time**—time is the *object* of the preposition **at.**
> **in the room**—room is the *object* of the preposition **in.**
> **on the way**—way is the *object* of the preposition **on.**
> **between you and me**—you and me are the *objects* of the preposition **between.**

In Lesson 8 you will be called upon to work with the *objects* of prepositions. For the moment let's just study the prepositions themselves. Here is a list of the most common prepositions. You undoubtedly know them all. But, did you know they are prepositions? Don't memorize this list but learn to recognize these words as prepositions.

> At, by, of, in, on, to, up, off, for, but, down, from, into, over, until, till, upon, with, about, above, after, along, among, below, since, under, across, before, behind, beyond, during, except, toward, within, without, around, beside, between, through, against, regarding, concerning, respecting, underneath, throughout, beneath.

In addition, there are a number of familiar word groups which are used as though the whole group were a preposition. Learn to recognize these word groups as prepositions.

> As to, as for, as regards, apart from, by way of, contrary to, devoid of, from out, from beyond, instead of, in place of, in regard to, in reference to, on account of, to the extent of, with respect to.

1. Using Prepositions

A. FROM AND THAN

Always use the word **from** after the word **different** when you mean that something is different from something else. It is *never* different **than** something else.

> Right: This may differ **from** what you had thought.
> Right: My theory is different **from** the one held by my brother.
> Right: Sing the song differently **from** the way you sang it last night.

B. AMONG AND BETWEEN

There is a difference of opinion (among) (between) you and me. **Between** is proper only when there are *two* people or things involved. **Among** is proper when there are *three or more*. Our sentence should read, **between you and me** . . . since there are only *two* people involved—you and me.

> Right: **Between** you and me, we have nothing to fear.
> Right: We shall place your display **among** the many others.
> Right: We shall place your display **between** the other two.

C. IN AND INTO

What is the difference between these two sentences?

1. The director is in the room.
2. The director went into the room.

In means **within**. **Into** means **from the outside to within**. In other words, **into** expresses an action of moving from one place (outside) to another place (inside). **In** expresses no action.

> The present is **in** the box.
> The child put his hand **into** the box to get the present.

D. OFF AND OF

Do not use the word **of** after the word **off**.

Right: The radio fell off the table. (NOT: The radio fell off of the table.)

Right: The letter dropped off the file.

Right: He is coming off the gangplank.

Do not use off of when you mean from.

Right: He borrowed the money from me. (NOT: He borrowed money off of me.)

Do not use of when you mean have. Remember: The word of never directly follows the word might, must, could, should, or would.

Right: I might have gone. (NOT: I might of gone.)

Right: I would have been there by now.

Right: I should have known this would happen.

E. Unnecessary Prepositions

You should avoid unnecessary prepositions that merely clutter your sentence without adding thought content.

1. Right: Where are you going? (NOT: Where are you going to?)
2. Right: Where is your home? (NOT: Where is your home at?)
3. Right: I cannot help expressing my gratitude. (NOT: I cannot help from expressing my gratitude.)
4. Right: I want you to see this. (NOT: I want for you to see this.)
5. Right: Until yesterday, I would have agreed. (NOT: Up until yesterday, I would have agreed.)
6. Right: In two weeks it will be over. (NOT: In two weeks it will be over with.)

2. The Right Preposition

As you have already seen, certain words call for one preposition and not another. You will be constantly using many such words in your work as a secretary. Below, is a list of words and their proper prepositions. Study this list carefully. Repeat each phrase over and over till it becomes familiar to your tongue and ear.

1. **Abide by** *(a decision.)*
   We hereby agree to **abide by** *the referee's decision.*

2. **Accompanied by** *(a person.)*
   Accompanied with *(an object.)*
   The President was **accompanied by** *the Vice President.*
   My order is **accompanied with** *my remittance.*

3. **Agree with** *(an opinion.)*
   Agree to *(terms.)*
   We **agree with** your *point of view* one-hundred percent.
   We **agree to** all the *terms* and conditions in the contract.

4. **Angry with** *(a person.)*
   Angry at *(an occurrence or object.)*
   I am extremely **angry with** *him.* (NOT: **at** him.)
   He became **angry at** the repeated *errors.*

5. **Comply with** (NOT: **to.**)
   It is our pleasure to **comply with** your request.
   Your **compliance with** this order will be required.

6. **Convenient to** *(a location.)*
   Convenient for *(a purpose.)*
   The home is **convenient to** all *shopping areas.*
   Is this date **convenient for** *holding* the fair?

7. **Correspond with** (means: *writing letters.*)
   Corresponds to (means: *equivalent.*)
   We are **corresponding with** a firm in Brazil.
   Does this layout **correspond to** your understanding?

8. **Differ from** *(a thing.)*
   Differ with *(an opinion.)*
   Our new *policy* **differs from** our former one in two respects.
   I am forced to **differ with** your *theory.*

Exercise 28

Recognizing Prepositions

This problem deals with recognizing prepositions. In each of the following sentences underline all prepositions with one line. Then underline the objects of those prepositions with two lines.

1. Did you hear of the trouble at the office?

2. Mr. Atwood was in his office when you called.

3. The reputation of Empire Fans has been built on high standards and fair dealings at all times.

4. Between you and me, I feel certain that one of the representatives will call at your office within a week.

5. In regard to any orders from your firm, we feel sure of our ability to fill them in time for your fall shipment.

6. Respecting your claim for damages, we are certain of a recovery to the extent of $3,000.

7. Contrary to our expectations, you will be refused a passport during the duration of the present emergency.

8. They have agreed among themselves to honor, without any question, all of the demands made by our client.

Exercise 29

Using Prepositions

A. This problem deals with the use of *from* after the word *different*. In the space provided write the proper preposition.

1. My idea is different _____from_____ yours.

2. Our course may differ _____ what you had expected.

3. Approach the topic differently _____ the way you did last time.

4. Our new line is a little different _____ last year's.

5. His designs are no different _____ the designs he showed last time.

6. It is hardly different _____ the plan I outlined.

7. The course they chose was different _____ that outlined in the manual.

B. In the space provided write either *among* or *between* whichever is correct.

1. There is a difference of opinion _____between_____ the two men.

2. There is a difference of opinion _____ the jury.

3. The Big Three often differ _____ themselves.

4. Chicago is _____ New York and Seattle.

5. _____ the people present were the President, the Vice-President and the Secretary of State.

6. The jewelry was found _____ his belongings.

7. _____ you and me, this plan will be a huge success.

8. _____ the reasons for his success were his wisdom, honesty, and fairness.

C. In the space provided write either *in* or *into*, whichever is correct.

1. He walked _____into_____ the room from the hall.

2. Behind a closed door, he paced back and forth _____ his office all day.

3. There are all sorts of articles _____ today's newspaper.

4. It doesn't take much to get _____ a fight with him.

5. What sort of work would you like to get _____?

6. Promotion is rapid, once you have established a name _____ this field.

7. He opened the door and rushed _____ his office.

8. I would tear this contract _____ a thousand little pieces if I could.

D. In the space provided, write the proper word or words.

1. Money was stolen (off of, from) the safe.   1. _____from_____

2. They took the receipts (off of, from) me.   2. _____

3. He borrowed money (off of, from) John.   3. _____

4. The idol has toppled (off of, from) its pedestal.   4. _____

5. I stepped (off of, from) the moving car.   5. _____

6. The child fell (off of, off) the chair.   6. _____

7. We all got (off of, off) the elevator at the same floor. 7. _____

8. The shirt was almost ripped (off of, off) the crooner's back. 8. _____

Exercise 29 (continued)

9. I could (have, of) completed the job by noon.

9. _____

10. They should (have, of) known he was lying.

10. _____

11. With luck he might (have, of) pulled through.

11. _____

12. They could (have, of) made many changes (among, between) the three of them.

12. _____

_____

13. He would (have, of) had very different opinions (from, than) mine.

13. _____

_____

14. When you went (in, into) this field you should (have, of) been prepared for a life very different (from, than) college life.

14. _____

_____

15. Standing (between, among) his brothers, John and Bob, he would (have, of) looked very different (from, than) either of them.

15. _____

_____

Exercise 30

The Proper Preposition

This problem deals with recognizing the proper preposition for a given word. In the space provided, write the preposition that best completes the thought. This problem not only reviews material in the text but will introduce you to the correct use of other prepositions.

1. Abide ___by___ a referee's decision.

2. Accompanied _____ his boss.

3. Accompanied _____ a remittance in full.

4. Agree _____ the terms of the contract.

5. Agree _____ his views on politics.

6. Agree _____ this method of attack.

7. Angry _____ the superintendent.

8. Angry _____ the rainy weather.

9. Comply _____ your request.

10. Convenient _____ all trains.

11. Convenient _____ all business needs.

12. Correspond _____ his firm by mail.

13. Correspond _____ my understanding.

14. Differ _____ his outlook on life.

15. Agree _____ the three of us.

16. Disappointed _____ the outcome.

17. Take advantage _____ an offer.

Exercise 30 (continued)

18. Deal _____ a problem.

19. Deal _____ stocks and bonds.

20. In contrast _____ other methods.

21. To contrast _____ other methods.

22. Abide _____ our decision.

23. Acquainted _____ the facts.

24. Agree _____ the two of us.

25. Provide _____ future needs.

26. Equivalent _____ a full gallon.

27. Emerge _____ the depths of despair.

28. Labor _____ pleasant conditions.

29. Labor _____ an understanding employer.

30. Labor _____ a difficult task.

31. A necessity _____ promptness.

32. Inseparable _____ one another.

33. In accordance _____ the vast majority.

34. Familiar _____ the entire process.

35. An exception _____ the rule.

36. Borrow _____ a friend.

37. Lend _____ a friend.

38. Accompanied _____ a cash payment.

39. Agree _____ the terms.

40. Indifferent _____ others.

41. Inquire _____ one's neighbor.

42. In contrast _____ his former work.

43. Accede _____ his wishes.

44. Angry _____ the drop in sales.

45. Conversant _____ all details.

46. Agree _____ a plan of attack.

47. Adapted _____ your needs.

48. Talk _____ his audience.

49. Adhere _____ my previous decision.

50. Distinguish _____ the two methods.

51. Comply _____ orders from headquarters.

52. Different _____ other methods.

53. Consist _____ wood and metal.

54. Enter _____ an agreement.

55. Impose _____ your neighbors.

56. Insight _____ complex matters.

57. Profit _____ former mistakes.

58. Coincide _____ the plans of others.

59. Approve _____ his behavior.

60. Dispense _____ all formality.

61. Correspond _____ air mail.

62. Capable _____ doing a fine job.

63. Depend _____ his parents.

64. Correspond _____ a friend overseas.

65. Accompanied _____ his mother.

66. Attend _____ business.

67. Conscious _____ the risks involved.

68. Appropriate _____ the occasion.

69. Participate _____ games.

70. Confide _____ his brother.

71. Correspond _____ his understanding.

72. Entertained _____ the comedian.

73. Identical _____ the original.

74. Confer _____ your doctor.

75. According _____ our contract.

76. In accordance _____ our contract.

77. Prohibited _____ doing an illegal act.

78. Concur _____ an opinion.

79. Abide _____ the court's ruling.

80. Depend _____ your wits.

81. Angry _____ his employee.

82. Proceed _____ the current plan.

83. Accompanied _____ invoices.

84. Absolve _____ all guilt.

85. Abstain _____ voting.

86. Convenient _____ buses and trolleys.

87. To object _____ certain conditions.

88. Different _____ his neighbor.

89. Agree _____ your opinion.

90. Participate _____ a contest.

91. Comply _____ your requests.

92. Correspond _____ our picture of events.

93. In contrast _____ other products.

94. Disagree _____ our opponents.

95. Differs _____ our old desk.

96. Disgusted _____ his boss.

97. In compliance _____ your order.

98. Differs _____ his boss.

99. Choose _____ the two.

100. Correspond _____ telegram.

MORE ABOUT PRONOUNS

"Me Tarzan. Me king of Jungle."

A movie script may sound like that, but your daily conversation had better not. Undoubtedly, you use the pronouns **I** and **me** properly most of the time, which is more than we can say for Tarzan. You automatically say:

> **I** want it. NOT: **Me** want it.
> Give it to **me**. NOT: Give it to **I**.

But in complicated sentences, your choice may become more difficult. Try this sentence, for example:

> **He thought it was (I) (me) who had started the car.**

Do you know whether **I** or **me** is correct? Do you know how to distinguish between the use of **he** and **him**, **she** and **her**, **we** and **us**, or **they** and **them**? Do you know when to use **who** and when to use **whom**? If you use these words properly at all times, you are a rare and fortunate person. In fact, you are a genius, and we would advise you not to read further in this lesson. However, if you are an ordinary mortal like the rest of us you will occasionally have difficulty choosing the proper pronoun, and this lesson is designed for you. We're going to show you how to make the choice of pronouns easy.

1. Types of Pronouns

Look at these sentences. They show you when to use **me** rather than **I**.

1. **Give it to me.** (Me is the *object* of the preposition, **to**.)
2. **He thanked me.** (Me is the *object* of the verb, **thanked**.)

Learn this simple rule: Always use **me**, not **I**, when the pronoun is the *object* of a preposition, or the *object* of a verb. In fact, **me** is called the **objective** form of the pronoun **I**. Similarly, **him** is the objective form of **he**, **her** is the objective form of **she**, **us** is the objective form of **we**, and **them** is the objective form of **they**.

Give it to him .... to her .... to us .... to them.

He thanked him .... thanked her .... thanked us .... thanked them.

Quickie Review: What should you know about *objective* pronouns? Only these two simple points!

1. The *objective* pronouns are: **me, him, her, us, them.**
2. You use *objective* pronouns as *objects* of verbs or objects of prepositions.

You may be wondering when to use the pronouns **I, he, she, we,** and **they.** Do these examples answer your question? Certainly these sentences are familiar.

1. **I want to go.** (I is the *subject* of the sentence.)
2. **It is I.** (I follows the *linking* verb **is.**)

That's all there is to it. Use **I, he, she, we,** or **they:**

1. as the *subject* of a sentence;
2. after a *linking* verb.

I want to go. He .... She .... We .... They want to go.

It is I. It is he. It is she. It is we. It is they.

NEVER: It is me.

Do you know the subject of a sentence when you see it? If not, review Lesson 1 on the parts of a sentence, at once. Do you know a linking verb when you see one? You should by now. You studied linking verbs in Lessons 4 and 6. Review those lessons right now if you are at all uncertain of linking verbs.

Quick Review: What should you know about the pronouns **I, he, she, we, they?** Remember these two points:

1. Use **I, he, she, we,** or **they** as the *subject* of a sentence.
2. Use **I, he, she, we,** or **they** after a *linking* verb.

Now, look again at the problem sentence you had at the beginning of this lesson.

He thought it was (I) (me) who had started the car.

98

Isn't this sentence easy now? The pronoun (**I**, or **me**) comes after the *linking* verb **was**. After a linking verb what do we use? That's right! **I**. Therefore:

He thought it was I who had started the car.

Simple, isn't it? (If it isn't, you had better reread this lesson.)

Let's take a few more difficult sentences. We'll show you how to make them easy. How would you complete this sentence:

1. **The invoice was sent by John and (I) (me).**

You would have no trouble if the sentence read:

2. **The invoice was sent by (I) (me).**

By just reading Sentence 2 aloud, you would hear that **me** is correct.

The invoice was sent by <u>me</u>.

In Sentence 1, ignore the word **John,** and use the same pronoun you would use if the pronoun were alone.

The invoice was sent by (John and) me.

Remember this simple rule: Use the same form of a pronoun when it is joined with another pronoun or a noun that you would use if the pronoun were alone.

Look at these examples:

1. **I** will move.
   (Bob and) **I** will move.
2. **He** is an expert. **I** am an expert.
   He and **I** are experts.
3. Did you know it was **he?** (After *linking* verb.)
   Did you know it was (Bob and) **he?**
4. The order was sent to **me.**
   The order was sent to (John and) **me.**
5. The report interests **me.**
   The report interests (John and) **me.**
6. Send **me** the folder.
   Send (John and) **me** the folder.

2. Using Pronouns

A. US AND WE

Here's a tricky sentence:

(We) (us) secretaries have interesting work.

To solve this problem-sentence, merely leave out the word *secretaries*.

(We) (us) have interesting work.

Answer: **We have interesting work.**

Therefore: **We secretaries have interesting work.**

Here are some similar examples:

1. The prize was given to (we) (us) girls.
   Omit **girls.** The prize was given to **us.** (NOT: . . . to **we.**)
   Therefore: The prize was given to **us** girls.
2. The director asked (us) (we) boys to be present.
   The director asked **us** . . . . (NOT: asked **we.**)
   Therefore: The director asked **us** boys to be present.
3. (We) (us) students should be cheerful and efficient.
   We should be . . . (NOT: **us** should be.)
   Therefore: **We** students should be cheerful and efficient.

B. THAN AND AS

1. **She is a better stenographer than (I, me.)**
2. **She was not so good as (he, him).**

Here's a simple trick that will make it easy for you to choose the proper pronoun after **than** or **as.** Add a little word that completes the meaning of such a sentence—a word such as **am, do,** or **was.**

For example:

1. **She is a better stenographer than (I, me.)** This means:
   She is a better stenographer than (I, me) am.
   Answer: . . . . **I** am. NOT: **me** am.
   Therefore: She is a better stenographer than **I.**
2. **She was not so good as (he, him.)** This means:

She was not so good as (he, him) was.

Answer: . . . . **He was.** NOT: him was.

Therefore: She was not so good as **he.**

3. **She does a better job than (I, me).** This means:

She does a better job than **I** (do).

4. **He would rather eat with John than (me, I.)** This means:

He would rather eat with John than (with) **me.**

C. BETWEEN YOU AND ME

Between you and (I, me), there's nothing to worry about.

If you remember from Chapter 6 that **between** is a *preposition*, you know that **me** is correct. **Me** is the *object* of the preposition **between.** Always say, **between you and me**—*never*, between you and **I.**

Between you and me, I think this will work.

Between you and me, who do you think will win?

3. Who—Whom

Whom is the *objective* form of the pronoun **who.** Therefore, you immediately know that you use **whom** as:

1. The *object* of a verb.
2. The *object* of a preposition.

You use **who:**

1. As the *subject* of a sentence.
2. After a *linking* verb.

Many secretaries find the choice of **who** or **whom** difficult. But, here's a trick that will make this choice *easy* for you. Whenever you have to choose between **who** and **whom** merely substitute **he** or **him.**

If **he** fits, **who** is correct.

If **him** fits, **whom** is correct.

Remember:

He = Who

Him = Whom

Note the **m** in both **him** and **whom.**

Let's try some examples:

1. (**Who, Whom**) is it?
   Substitute **he** or **him.**
   He is it. NOT: **Him** is it.
   Therefore:
   Who is it?
2. It is (**who, whom?**)
   Substitute:
   It is he. NOT: It is **him.**
   Therefore:
   It is who?

3. (**Who, Whom**) do you want?
Substitute, and place **he** or **him** at the end of the question for the sake of clarity:
   Do you want him? NOT: Do you want **he?**
   Therefore:
   Whom do you want?
4. **You were referring to** (**who, whom**)?
   Substitute:
   You were referring to him. NOT: You were referring to **he.**
   Therefore:
   You were referring to whom?
5. (**Who, Whom**) **threw the overalls into Mrs. Murphy's chowder?**
(You should know the answer to this one. Test it by substituting **he** or **him.**)
6. **He is a man** (**who, whom**) **is loved by all.**
This sentence can be broken into two parts, which we call clauses.
   a. **He is a man . . .**
   b. **. . .** (**who, whom**) **is loved by all.**
In such a sentence test **who** or **whom** in its own clause. Whichever form is correct in its own clause is correct in the entire sentence.
   Substitute:
   b. **. . . he is loved by all.** NOT: **him** is loved by all.

Therefore:

He is a man who is loved by all.

7. **He is a man (who, whom) we all love.**

This sentence also divides into two clauses.

    a. **He is a man . . .**

    b. **. . . (who, whom) we all love.**

Again we test **who** or **whom** in its own clause.

Substitute:

    b. **. . . we all love him.** NOT: we all love **he.**

Therefore:

He is a man whom we all love.

8. **There is an urgent need for men (who, whom) we can trust.**

Substitute:

    . . . we can trust him. NOT: **he.**

9. **He is a man (who, whom) I am positive can be trusted.**

Do not let **I am positive** fool you. Always disregard expressions such as, **I think, I believe, I am certain, I am positive, did you say,** when they follow **who** or **whom.**

This sentence can be broken into:

    a. **He is a man . . .**

    b. **. . . (who, whom) can be trusted.**

    c. Disregard **I am positive.**

Substitute:

He can be trusted. NOT: **Him** can be trusted.

Therefore:

He is a man who I am positive can be trusted.

10. **(Who, Whom) did you say was at the door?**

(Analyze this sentence by ignoring **did you say.**)

Substitute:

He was at the door. NOT: **Him** was at the door.

Therefore:

Who did you say was at the door.

11. **The man (who, whom) I think will be our next president will be here soon.**

Break this sentence down as follows:

    a. **The man . . . will be here soon.**

    b. **. . . (who, whom) will be our next president.**

    c. Disregard **I think.**

Substitute in its own clause:

He will be our next president. NOT: **him will be . . . .**

Therefore:

The man who I think will be our next president will be here soon.

12. **The man (who, whom) I believe we all love is standing next to me.**

    a. **The man . . . is standing next to me.**

    b. **. . . (who, whom) we all love . . . .**

    c. Disregard **I believe.**

Substitute in its own clause:

We all love him. NOT: **We all love he.**

Therefore:

The man whom I believe we all love is standing next to me.

4. Whoever and Whomever

Whomever is the objective form of **whoever.** Once again we can use our trick and make the choice easy. Disregard all words in the sentence before **whoever** or **whomever.** Then substitute:

Substitute **he** for **whoever.**

Substitute **him** for **whomever.**

1. **(Whoever, Whomever) answers the phone should be pleasant.**

Substitute:

He answers the phone. NOT: **Him answers the phone.**

Therefore:

Whoever answers the phone should be pleasant.

2. **Give the prize to (whoever, whomever) you please.**

Disregard all words in the sentence before **whoever** or **whomever.**

Disregard: **Give the prize to.**

Substitute:

You please him. NOT: **You please he.**

Therefore:

Give the prize to whomever you please.

3. **Give the prize to (whoever, whomever) deserves it.**

   Disregard: **Give the prize to.**

   Substitute:

   He deserves it. NOT: **Him** deserves it.

Therefore:

Give the prize to whoever deserves it.

4. **She always accepts help from (whoever, whomever) will give it.**

   Substitute in its own clause:

   He will give it. NOT: **Him** will give it.

Therefore:

She always accepts help from whoever will give it.

Exercise 31

Review Preparation

A. This is a review problem dealing with action and linking verbs. In each of the following sentences is an italicized verb. In the space provided mark A if it is an action verb; mark L if it is a linking verb.

1. It *would have been* easier had we been better prepared.
2. Can we *expect* you before noon?
3. It *became* difficult for him to work.
4. He *tasted* the food with gusto.
5. Things *look* bad for the moment.
6. He *lay* down to rest.
7. It *sounded* like a good idea.
8. He *rose* at dawn.
9. This *is* the truth.
10. *Was* it he who met you?

1. ___L___
2. _____
3. _____
4. _____
5. _____
6. _____
7. _____
8. _____
9. _____
10. _____

B. This is a review problem that deals with the objects of verbs and the objects of prepositions. Underline each *object* of a verb or of a preposition in the following sentences. Write OV above the word if it is the object of a verb; write OP above the word if it is the object of a preposition.

1. John still loves Mary.
              OV above Mary

2. All of the men were dissatisfied with the wage offer.

3. It seemed to him that all was lost.

4. Send the books to us by fast mail.

5. Thank you for your kind cooperation.

6. We should like to place a definite order for holiday goods.

7. This is no time for him to leave the firm.

8. This is how we know when to start the machine.

9. We shall have our fall order ready for delivery as soon as we get word from our buyer.

10. We explained to your salesman that we did not want the shoes before August because we have our annual sale during July.

Exercise 32

Pronouns

A. This problem deals with the different forms a pronoun can take. In the space provided write the objective form and the possessive forms of each pronoun.

	Objective Form	Possessive Forms	
1. I	me	my	mine
2. you	_____	_____	_____
3. he	_____	_____	_____
4. she	_____	_____	_____
5. it	_____	_____	_____
6. we	_____	_____	_____
7. they	_____	_____	_____

B. This problem deals with the use of the pronoun as the subject of a sentence. In the space provided write the correct pronoun. These problems should be easy.

1. (I, me) am extremely pleased with his progress.   1. ___I___

2. (He, Him) is an exceptionally gifted salesman.   2. _____

3. Last night, (us, we) went to the theater after dinner.   3. _____

4. In the long run (her, she) will undoubtedly succeed.   4. _____

5. Contrary to our advice, (them, they) all agreed to the resolution.   5. _____

Exercise 32 (continued)

6. During our last convention, (we, us) presented the new idea.   6. _____

7. To preserve our position as leader in our field, (I, me) propose a new concept.   7. _____

8. In the beginning, (she, her) was uncertain of her duties.   8. _____

9. Up to the present, (he, him) has the best selling record.   9. _____

10. Despite their opposition, (them, they) agreed to abide by our decision.   10. _____

11. (Us, We) are certain (us, we) can stop their gains.   11. _____

12. If it were up to me, (I, me) would tell them that either (them, they) work with us or (us, we) take drastic action.   12. _____

C. This problem deals with the form of the pronoun after a linking verb. In the space provided, write the proper pronoun.

1. It is (I, me.)   1. ___I___

2. It is (he, him.)   2. _____

3. It is (her, she.)   3. _____

4. It is (us, we.)   4. _____

5. It is (them, they.)   5. _____

6. It was (I, me.)   6. _____

7. It was (he, him.)   7. _____

8. It was (her, she.)   8. _____

9. It was (us, we.)   9. _____

10. It was (them, they.)   10. _____

11. I thought it was (he, him.)   11. _____

12. I thought it was (her, she.)   12. _____

13. I thought it was (them, they.)   13. _____

14. It was (he, him) who sent the order.   14. _____

15. If it was (he, him) who sent the order, (he, him) should be congratulated.   15. _____

16. The last person to leave was (her, she.)   16. _____

17. The winners of the award were (them, they.)   17. _____

18. If I were (he, him) and he were (I, me), this would be a different world.   18. _____

19. It must have been (her, she) who delivered the message.   19. _____

20. That is (them, they) walking toward us.   20. _____

D. This problem deals with the use of the proper pronoun as the object of a verb. In the space provided, write the correct pronoun.

1. They hired (I, me) for the job.   1. ___me___

2. They hired (he, him) for the job.   2. _____

3. The decision shocked (he, him.)   3. _____

4. The explosion knocked (her, she) out of her chair.   4. _____

5. In the end, he lent (us, we) his support.   5. _____

6. Send (them, they) the letters at once.   6. _____

7. Permit (I, me) to voice my disapproval.   7. _____

8. You have told (us, we) a most fascinating story.   8. _____

9. They would not allow (he, him) to leave.   9. _____

10. The director told (us, we) that his decision had been reached.   10. _____

E. This problem deals with the use of the proper pronoun as the object of a preposition. In the space provided, write the correct pronoun.

1. The message was sent to (I, me.)   1. ___me___

2. The message was sent by (he, him.)   2. _____

3. We had learned a great deal from (her, she.)   3. _____

4. The committee sent its congratulations to (us, we.)   4. _____

5. Mr. Smith walked right by (them, they) without even acknowledging their presence.   5. _____

6. He came directly to (I, me) for the information.   6. _____

7. They stared at (he, him) as he entered the room.   7. _____

8. The idea came to (them, they) at the same instant.   8. _____

9. The order was delivered directly to (us, we.)   9. _____

10. John stood between (I, me) and the door.   10. _____

Exercise 33

The Proper Pronoun I

A. This problem deals with the use of the proper pronoun. In the space provided write the correct pronoun.

Exercise 33 (continued)

1. The letter was sent directly to (he, him.)

2. We knew that (she, her) would accept the offer.

3. It was (I, me) who ordered the books from (they, them.)

4. Did you see (us, we) at the theater?

5. If I were (her, she), I would demand a raise.

6. Are you certain that (they, them) will not accept your invitation?

7. Was it (he, him) who spoke to the representative?

8. Deliver this message to (they, them) at once.

9. Permit (I, me) to differ with (he, him.)

10. Stop (I, me) if you've heard this.

1. _____him_____
2. _____
3. _____
4. _____
5. _____
6. _____
7. _____
8. _____
9. _____
10. _____

B. This problem deals with the use of the proper pronoun when it is joined with another pronoun or a noun. Fill in the correct pronoun in the space provided. Remember, use the same pronoun you would use if it were alone.

1. Bob and (he, him) will go.

2. The men congratulated Mr. Robinson and (I, me.)

3. Mr. Smith will introduce you and (he, him) to the staff.

4. Our office is certain that you and (her, she) will get the job.

5. (He, Him) and (I, me) will leave on the early train.

6. They gave raises in salary to (he, him) and (I, me.)

7. The winners of the prizes were (he, him) and (her, she.)

8. Between you and (I, me), this is a dangerous proposition.

9. The salesmen in your territory are Mr. Johnson and (I, me.)

10. The boys and (I, me) feel certain that the contract will be awarded to you and (they, them.)

1. _____he_____
2. _____
3. _____
4. _____
5. _____
6. _____
7. _____
8. _____
9. _____
10. _____

Exercise 34

The Proper Pronoun II

This is an over-all problem dealing with choosing the proper pronoun. In the space provided write the correct pronoun.

1. Give it to (he, him.)

2. (He, Him) likes this method of accounting.

3. This will shock (he, him.)

1. _____him_____
2. _____
3. _____

4. It was (he, him) who started the trouble.   4. _____

5. This message is for (she, her.)   5. _____

6. Here is a story that will astound (they, them.)   6. _____

7. Was it (I, me) you saw at the theater?   7. _____

8. Are you sure you sent (I, me) the bill?   8. _____

9. John and (he, him) are next on the list.   9. _____

10. Give the order to Charles and (he, him.)   10. _____

11. (We, Us) salesmen must plan our campaign carefully.   11. _____

12. (He and I) (Him and me) will leave at about dawn.   12. _____

13. Was it (he, him) you spoke to?   13. _____

14. The order directed (us, we) secretaries to come to work fifteen minutes earlier.   14. _____

15. He is not so clever as (I, me.)   15. _____

16. This man is a better salesman than (I, me.)   16. _____

17. He would rather work with John than (I, me.)   17. _____

18. Between you and (I, me), this work is easy.   18. _____

19. Mr. Roberts is as good a manager as (he, him.)   19. _____

20. It was (she, her) who cut the endowment fund.   20. _____

Exercise 35

Who and Whom

This problem deals with the choice of *who* or *whom*, *whoever* or *whomever*. In the space provided write the proper word. Remember, substitute: *He* = *who* or *whoever*; *Him* = *whom* or *whomever*.

1. (Who, Whom) is at the door?   1. _____who_____

2. It is (who, whom) that you want to meet?   2. _____

3. (Who, Whom) did you say called?   3. _____

4. Our choice is a man (who, whom) you all know.   4. _____

5. Our choice is a man (who, whom) is known by all.   5. _____

6. He likes (whoever, whomever) is kind to him.   6. _____

7. He is a man (who, whom) I think can be fully trusted in his position.   7. _____

8. (Who, Whom) were you speaking of?   8. _____

9. (Who, Whom) among you knows the answer?   9. _____

10. (Whomever, Whoever) gets there first wins the prize.   10. _____

11. He likes (whoever, whomever) he meets.   11. _____

12. She is a woman (who, whom) I feel confident we can rely on.   12. _____

13. Upon (who, whom) will you bestow the award?   13. _____

14. She is a person (who, whom) is most talented.   14. _____

15. She is a person (who, whom) we know to be talented.   15. _____

16. One man (who, whom) was chosen for accomplishment refused to take
    the job.   16. _____

17. Choose (whoever, whomever) you think best.   17. _____

18. It is the intelligent man (who, whom) succeeds.   18. _____

19. Have you determined (who, whom) you want for the job?   19. _____

20. Please tell me (who, whom) you think will win.   20. _____

Review Exercise
More About Pronouns

A number of pronouns in the following letter are misused. Cross out each incorrectly written pronoun and write the proper pronoun above it.

Dear Mr. Backrack:

I would like to tell you more about Robert Gilbert, the man ~~who~~ *whom* I started to describe to you last week. Mr. Gilbert is a man who is constantly employed in top executive positions. Ten years ago it was him and Bob Anthony whom raised the Eighth National Bank to its present position. It was him whom gave the Smith Company its shot in the arm. It was him whom the Jones Corporation called upon when it needed help.

There are few men such as him left in the business world. If it were left to I, I would definitely choose Robert Gilbert for the Presidency of this firm. He is a man whom I believe can lead us out of our present difficulty. He is a man whom I believe we can accept as a leader and inspiration. He is a man whom I believe will lead we to the top position in our field.

I am sure that whoever the Board chooses as President will do a fine job. However, I would choose Robert Gilbert. I cannot think of a man whom is better qualified, whom is more trustworthy, whom will do a better job, than him.

Respectfully,

Lesson 9

CONJUNCTIONS

A conjunction is the *glue* that holds one part of a sentence to another. Here is a list of some familiar conjunctions: **and, but, because, or, so then, yet, accordingly, besides, consequently, thus, therefore, moreover, hence, notwithstanding, as soon as, whereas, though, until, supposing, otherwise, in order that, inasmuch as.**

Conjunctions do more than just connect two ideas. The conjunction shows the *relationship* between ideas. As a secretary, use your conjunctions carefully so that they express the precise relationship you intend.

For example, in each of these sentences, which conjunction best shows the relationship between the ideas it connects:

1. **This book is heavy to carry, (and) (but) it is light reading.**
2. **This book is heavy, (and) (but) it is bulky, too.**

To convey the exact meaning intended in Sentence 1, **but** is proper. In Sentence 2, **and** is proper. Do you see why?

1. Using Conjunctions

A. PAIRS OF CONJUNCTIONS

Certain conjunctions act together to connect ideas.

1. **Either . . . or: Either** you work harder **or** you leave.
2. **Neither . . . nor:** We want **neither** sympathy **nor** charity.
3. **Both . . . and:** The true leader is **both** self-confident **and** humble.
4. **Not only . . . but also:** We **not only** want you to visit our office **but also** to inspect our plant.
5. **Whether . . . or: Whether** you act now **or** wait is a matter of great concern.

The major points to remember about these paired conjunctions are:

1. With **neither** always use **nor** (NOT: **or.**)
   We want neither sympathy nor charity.

2. With **not only** always use **but also** (NOT: **but alone.**)
We not only want you to visit our office but also to inspect our plant.

B. LIKE AND AS

Like and as are frequently used improperly. You won't make such an error if you remember this hint:
Use like only when you mean, **similar to.**
> **Right:** He looks like (similar to) me.
> **Right:** It was done as you wanted.

Remember, like is a preposition, not a conjunction.

C. TRY AND . . . .

This sentence is wrong: **You must try and do it.**
You should say: **You must try to do it.**

D. PROVIDED AND PROVIDING

Provided is a conjunction. **Providing** is *not* a conjunction and should never be used to join two parts of a sentence.

> **Right:** We will arrive on time, provided we have a tail-wind.
> **Right:** Provided there is time, you give your speech.
> **WRONG:** We will arrive on time, providing we have a tail-wind.

2. Interjections

Just one word about interjections. That's all they deserve. An interjection is a word or group of words that expresses strong feeling. Always follow an interjection with an *exclamation point.*

Good! Surprise! Well done! Oh! Magnificent!

Exercise 36
Using Conjunctions

A. This problem deals with choosing the proper conjunction. In the space provided write the correct word.

Exercise 36 (continued)

1. Either you ship the goods (or, and) I bring action.   1. _____or_____

2. Neither the chair (or, nor) the desk is in perfect condition.   2. _____

3. Both the fan (and, or) the motor were defective.   3. _____

4. He not only refused to accept the goods (but, but also) refused to pay.   4. _____

5. Whether prices go up (or, nor) go down, we will profit.   5. _____

6. Neither the dictionary (or, nor) the glossary included the term.   6. _____

7. He not only gave us dinner (but, but also) invited us to stay for the evening.   7. _____

8. Either your shipping department (or, nor) your order department was at fault.   8. _____

9. Whether we succeed (or, nor) not, we shall have tried.   9. _____

10. They are willing to offer you not only a discount (but, but also) a bonus gift.   10. _____

11. They offered either a straight salary (and, or) a commission.   11. _____

12. Our latest model is not only functional (but, but also) artistic.   12. _____

13. He was neither enthusiastic (and, nor) discouraging.   13. _____

14. Either the ledger (or, nor) the receipt (is, are) incorrect.   14. _____

15. Both the teacher (and, or) her students have responsibilities.   15. _____

B. This problem deals with choosing the proper conjunction. In the space provided, write the proper word.

1. I acted (as, like) you advised.   1. _____as_____

2. Would you try (and, to) correct the error?   2. _____

3. We will accept (provided, providing) you lower your price.   3. _____

4. We would appreciate it if you would try (and, to) locate the lost files.   4. _____

5. The calculator was fully (as, so) large as a room.   5. _____

6. We will not only go to Paris (but, but also) to London.   6. _____

7. This contract is valid (provided, providing) the shipment arrives on schedule.   7. _____

8. (Like, As) I said yesterday, this must stop.   8. _____

9. Neither time (or, nor) effort is to be spared, (provided, providing) they cooperate.   9. _____ _____

10. It looks very much (like, as) your automatic washer.   10. _____

Lesson 10

PUNCTUATION

Can you read this:

marksofpunctuationtellthereaderwhentopause

Now, try it this way:

Marks of punctuation tell the reader when to pause.

Easier, isn't it? What a difference a few little spaces make. These spaces make a sentence easier to read because they break a long mumble-jumble of letters into easy-to-understand words. In the same manner, marks of punctuation make sentences easier to read because they break a mumble-jumble of thoughts into easy-to-understand ideas.

If you want your writing to say exactly what you mean, you must learn to punctuate correctly and carefully. Improper punctuation will not only confuse the reader, but may completely mislead him. For example, see how a comma completely changes the meaning of this sentence:

> **No price too high.**
> **No, price too high.**

You, as a secretary, must be able to punctuate perfectly. So, study this section thoroughly and carefully. Your mastery of the rules of punctuation will pave your way to a high-paying position.

1. The Period (.)

The use of this mark of punctuation is very easy. You have probably used it properly throughout your life. Therefore, the four rules, below, should be a review for you.

RULE 1.

Place a period at the end of a sentence that makes a statement.

> **I shall go tomorrow.**
> **It rained in the morning.**
> **Mr. Jones is not at home.**

115

RULE 2.

Place a period at the end of a sentence that states a command.

> **Bring it here.**
> **Don't leave.**
> **Order the goods immediately.**

RULE 3.

Place a period after an abbreviation.

> **Mr.**   (Mister)
> **Dr.**   (Doctor)
> **N.Y.C.**   (New York City)
> **e.g.**   (for example)

NOTE: When a sentence ends with an abbreviation use only *one* period.

> **Address the letter to Jones, Inc.**
> **He lives in Atlanta, Ga.**

RULE 4.

Use a period to separate cents from dollars in a money amount.

> **$2.58**   **$10.00**   **$4,372.27**

2. The Question Mark (?)

The use of this mark, too, should be easy. You use the question mark in only one place—after a question.

> **Where can we get more material?**
> **Did you answer his letter?**
> **Who?**

NOTE 1: Do not use a question mark after a sentence such as this:

> **Will you please file this letter at once.**

This is not really a question. It is a *command* phrased in the form of a question for the sake of politeness. As you just learned, a command ends with a *period*.

> **Will you please let me hear from you in the very near future.**
> **Won't you come in, please.**

NOTE 2: The question mark usually ends a sentence. However, on rare occasions it may be used in the middle of a sentence and no capital letter need follow it.

> Can you name four Presidents? four Vice-Presidents? four Chief Justices?

3. The Exclamation Point (!)

Here's the mark of punctuation that's simplest to use. *Use the exclamation point after an exclamation*—that is, after a word of strong feeling or emotion:

> Hurrah!
> No!
> Eureka!
> That's life!
> What a wonderful day!

4. The Comma (,)

Do you use commas correctly at all times? About a hundred years ago the use of the comma was a great problem. You see, at that time each writer punctuated as he pleased. The result was almost a competition between authors to see who could write the most obscure sentences. The literary style of the day favored long, complicated, tedious sentences, besplattered with commas and semi-colons. It was left to the poor reader to unravel this cobweb of confusion as best he could.

Thank heavens, times have changed. Today the tendency is toward short simple sentences and easy-to-follow punctuation. Today it is a serious error to use too many commas. You must have a definite reason for every comma you insert. It you don't have a reason, leave it out. Remember this about the comma:

WHEN IN DOUBT, LEAVE IT OUT.

There really aren't many rules governing the use of the commas. In fact, we can break the use of the comma into only six easy-to-master rules—rules that you probably know already.

For example, you probably know that you use commas to separate items listed in a series.

RULE 1.

Use the comma to separate items listed in a series.

117

We have a large supply of wool, rayon, nylon, and silk.

We have plants in New York, Los Angeles, Dallas, and Seattle.

Our objectives are to learn to write, to speak, and to think well.

That you are aggressive, that you are clever, and that you are successful are facts we cannot deny.

NOTE 1. Note that a comma is placed before the **and** that precedes the last word in the series. This is the modern rule of punctuation.

Mr. Smith, Mr. Jones, and Mr. Brown will be pleased to attend.

The Brown Printing Co. will print our books, supplies, and posters.

NOTE 2. You may omit all commas if conjunctions are used to connect the items of a series.

Deliver the books and the paper and the boxes.

To write and to speak and to think well are your objectives in this course.

NOTE 3. Use commas to separate a list of words that *describe* one particular thing. Do *not* place a comma after the last word in such a list

Luscious, plump, golden-hued pears are on sale downtown.

Our building gives a tall, stately appearance.

Mr. Smith is an energetic, alert, shrewd businessman.

NOTE 4. Use a comma after the last word in a series when the series is followed by a complete statement.

Tables, chairs, desks, and lamps, all are yours for the asking.

Courage, fortitude, and wisdom, these are the strength of our nation.

BUT: Courage, fortitude, and wisdom are the strength of our nation.

RULE 2.

Use commas to set off expressions that if omitted would not destroy the sentence nor change its meaning. This rule covers a great variety of situations. To make it easier for you to apply Rule 2, we shall break it down into individual parts. But don't forget, they are all part of the *one* over-all rule.

PART A.

Use commas to set off the name of a person directly addressed.

Mr. Smith, we know that you will cooperate.

We can omit **Mr. Smith** and still have a complete sentence.

> Omit: **Mr. Smith**
> Remainder: **We know that you will cooperate.**

Therefore, we set off **Mr. Smith** with a comma.

Notice that the name of the person addressed is set off with commas no matter where it appears in the sentences.

> **Mr. Smith, we know that you will cooperate.**
> **We know, Mr. Smith, that you will cooperate.**
> **We know that you will cooperate, Mr. Smith.**

NOTE 1. When the name of the person addressed occurs in the middle of the sentence, place a comma before and after the name.

> **On your honor, John, did you do it?**
> **With your help, Mr. Jones, we cannot fail.**

NOTE 2. This rule applies only to the name of a person who is directly addressed. If you are talking *about* someone, you don't set off his name with commas.

> **Smith is a good man.**
> BUT: **Smith, you are a good man.**

NOTE 3. Use commas when you directly address someone with a term other than his name.

> **You, my friend, are in for a surprise.**
> **Let me tell you, fellow alumnus, what the committee has done.**

PART B.

Use commas to set off an expression that explains a preceding word.

1. Mr. Jones, President of Acme Steel, is here.

President of Acme Steel merely explains who **Mr. Jones** is. We could omit it and still have a full sentence unchanged in meaning.

> Omit: **President of Acme Steel**
> Remainder: **Mr. Jones is here.**

2. The Pacific Ocean, largest body of water on earth, must be protected by a vast naval system.

> Omit: **largest body of water on earth.**
>
> Remainder: **The Pacific Ocean must be protected by a vast naval system.**

3. We will send Mr. Smith, our representative, to visit your office.

> Omit: **our representative**
>
> Remainder: **We will send Mr. Smith to visit your office.**

4. The company, having been dormant for years, is finally reawakening.

> Omit: **having been dormant for years**
>
> Remainder: **The company is finally reawakening.**

5. Our firm will show you how, merely by changing your circulars, you can double your business.

> Omit: **merely by changing your circulars**
>
> Remainder: **Our firm will show you how you can double your business.**

6. Butter that is rancid is sickening.

> Omit: **that is rancid**
>
> Remainder: **Butter is sickening.**

Do we actually mean that **butter is sickening?** NO! Only certain butter —rancid butter—is sickening. Go back and look at Rule 2 again. It says that we use commas to set off expressions that if omitted would not destroy the sentence *nor change its meaning.* **That is rancid** is *essential* to the meaning of our sentence. Therefore, it should *not* be set off by commas.

> **Butter that is rancid is sickening.**

7. Butter, which is in great demand, is selling well.

> Omit: **which is in great demand**
>
> Remainder: **Butter is selling well.**

Do we mean to say that **butter is selling well?** Yes. Therefore, the use of commas is proper since the expression **which is in great demand** is *not* necessary to the meaning of the sentence.

8. Air that is polluted is bad for you.
   Omit: **that is polluted**
   Remainder: **Air is bad for you.**

Do we mean that **air is bad for you?** NO! Only **polluted air** is bad for you. Therefore, **that is polluted** should not be set off with commas since it is essential to the meaning of the sentence.

9. The men in our office, who won the prize, shall get a bonus.
   Omit: **who won the prize**
   Remainder: **The men in our office shall get a bonus.**

The use of commas here is correct if *all* the men in the office won the prize. The Remainder tells us that *all* the men in the office shall get bonuses. Suppose that the men in our office won a bowling contest against the men in another office. Then the use of commas in this sentence is correct.

However, suppose there were a bowling contest in which each man was on his own. Some men in the office won and others did not. In such a case we would not use commas.

The men in our office who won the prize shall get a bonus.

In this case, **who won the prize** is essential to the meaning of the sentence since it tells us exactly which men get bonuses.

NOTE 1. Here's a little test of what you learned thus far. See how omitting a comma changes the meaning of these two sentences:

1. **Mr. Jones, our salesman, will see you.**
2. **Mr. Jones, our salesman will see you.**

Do you see the difference in meaning? In Sentence 1, the salesman, whose name is **Jones**, will see you. In Sentence 2, *your* name is **Jones** and you will be seen by a salesman whose name we don't know. Let this be an object lesson that you must place your commas carefully.

121

Part C.

Use commas to separate a connective such as **therefore, nevertheless, in fact, however, of course,** naturally, *from the body of the sentence.*

1. We feel, therefore, that you must act with caution.
   Omit: **therefore**
   Remainder: **We feel that you must act with caution.**

2. It was, nevertheless, important to hear his statement.
   Omit: **nevertheless**
   Remainder: **It was important to hear his statement.**

3. There was little we could do, of course.
   Omit: **of course.**
   Remainder: **There was little we could do.**

NOTE 1. Some other expressions which are generally set off by commas are: on the other hand, at any rate, for example, as a matter of fact, as we understand it.

> On the other hand, we can do no more than wait.
> We feel, at any rate, that some adjustment should be made.
> Look at the results in June, for example.
> As a matter of fact, we were importing steel in June.
> The key to this matter, as we understand it, is the exchange rate.

Part D.

Use a comma to set off a question that is added to a statement.

1. You sent the letter, did you not?
   Omit: **did you not?**
   Remainder: **You sent the letter.**

2. Lovely day, isn't it?
   Omit: **isn't it?**
   Remainder: **Lovely day.**

3. You will do as we ask, won't you?
   Omit: **won't you?**
   Remainder: **You will do as we ask.**

122

PART E.

*Use a comma to set off an opposing idea beginning with **not**.*

1. Mr. Smith has gone to Chicago, not to St. Louis.

   Omit: **not to St. Louis.**

   Remainder: **Mr. Smith has gone to Chicago.**

2. The motor is hot, not cool.

   Omit: **not cool.**

   Remainder: **The motor is hot.**

3. What this nation wants is peace, not war.

   Omit: **not war.**

   Remainder: **What this nation wants is peace.**

RULE 3.

Use a comma to set off a short quotation from the rest of the sentences.

> He said, "I will not budge an inch."
> "Do unto others as you would have others do unto you," is the Golden Rule.
> "Send the bills at once," he threatened, "or there will be trouble around here."

NOTE 1. When the quotation is not direct and not in quotation marks, no comma is necessary.

> He said that he would not budge.
> The golden rule says that we should do unto others as we would have them do unto us.

NOTE 2. When the quotation is not a complete thought in itself but is a necessary part of the entire sentence, you omit the comma.

> He said he was "extremely humiliated."
> The summer days are "dog days."

RULE 4.

*Use a comma to separate two complete thoughts that are connected by conjunctions such as **but, and, or.***

123

Do you remember, from the section on Run-on Sentences, that these conjunctions are used as *glue* to hold two complete thoughts together in one sentence? Review that section on Run-on Sentences *now*. It will make this Rule 4 much easier.

> We hope to attend the banquet, but we may be detained by business.
> Mr. Jackson took the 5:15 train, and he should be here any minute.
> You must accept our offer, or you will suffer the consequences.

NOTE 1. Note that in each of the foregoing examples the comma comes before the conjunction. There is no comma after the conjunction.

NOTE 2. In a short sentence you may omit the comma if the meaning of the sentence is clear. As a rule of thumb, if either part of the sentence is *five* words or less you may omit the comma.

> Your order arrived and we shipped it.
> The bell rang but we remained in our seats because of the teacher's instructions.

NOTE 3. You should know what's wrong with the use of the comma in this sentence:

> WRONG: We must change our advertising appeal, we may lose large part of our market.

If you have reviewed the section on Run-on Sentences, you can correct this sentence easily.

> Right: We must change our advertising appeal. We may lose a large part of our market.
> Right: We must change our advertising appeal, <u>or</u> we may lose a large part of our market.

RULE 5.

In the section on Sentence Fragments in Lesson 1 you learned about a

124

type of expression that contains a subject and predicate, but by itself does not express complete thought. For example:

Since the order arrived . . . .

Stop! You will find it very difficult to understand the following section unless you review the section on Sentence Fragments. Only when you are fully familiar with the contents of that section, should you proceed.

Do you understand the *dependent clause* now? All right, then let's proceed.

When a sentence *begins* with a dependent clause, you should separate that clause from the rest of the sentence with a comma. Observe the following examples:

Since the order arrived, we have made headway.
As soon as we heard the news, we ran to congratulate you.
Because we failed to get the part, we left the theater.

However, when a sentence *ends* with a dependent clause, you generally should NOT use a comma.

We have made headway **since the order arrived.**
We ran to congratulate you **as soon as we heard the news.**
We left the theater **because we failed to get the part.**

Similarly, when a sentence begins with a dependent expression such as:

Coming to the end of the day . . . .

you should separate this expression from the rest of the sentence with a comma. For example:

Coming to the end of the day, we still had not finished.
Hurrying to the best of our ability, we arrived on time.
Prices having gone up, we had to cut our purchases.

RULE 6.

Use commas in writing: a. *large numbers;* b. *dates;* c. *addresses;* d. *proper names with last names first; e. the complimentary close of a letter.*

a. Numbers: *Use commas to separate numbers into groups of three.*

> The national debt is over $270,000,000,000.00.
> Ship 1,250 cards, at once.

b. Dates: *In a sentence, place a comma before and after the year.*

> Your order of July 8, 1956, arrived safely.

c. Addresses: *Use the comma to separate parts of an address, as follows:*

> John Jones
> 1776 Broadway
> Atlanta, Georgia
> Mr. Jones lives at 1776 Broadway, Atlanta, Georgia.

d. Names: *When writing a proper name with last name first, separate the names with commas.*

> Jones, John Paul
> BUT: John Paul Jones

e. Letters: *Use a comma after the complimentary close of a letter.*

> Sincerely,
> Very truly yours,
> Respectfully,

5. The Colon (:)

The colon is an easy mark of punctuation. You use it in only four, simple ways.

RULE 1.

Use the colon after the complimentary salutation of a business letter.

> Dear Madam:
> Gentlemen:

RULE 2.

Use the colon to introduce a long, formal quotation. Remember, you use a comma before a short, informal quotation.

126

Senator Jones replied as follows: "I know the importance of this investigation, but I would be ill-advised to become a party to such a circus."

Rule 3.

Use the colon to introduce a long list or tabulation.

Here is what we have on hand: one hammer, three screw drivers, one clipper.
Mail the following invoices: #3721, #3722, #3723, #3724.

Rule 4.

Use colons to separate hours from minutes.

The train departs at 6:43 a.m. and arrives at 5:06 p.m.

6. The Semicolon (;)

The semi-colon is a mark of punctuation that is very unpopular these days. If you use semi-colons frequently, this indicates that your sentences are long, complicated, and probably unclear. The most important rule that you should learn about the semi-colon is to *leave it out*. Rather than write a long complicated sentence, break it into two small, separate sentences. Always use a *period* rather than a semi-colon, if it is at all possible.

However, this does not mean that you can ignore the rules of semi-colon punctuation. As a secretary you cannot always choose your boss, nor can you teach him good English if he doesn't already know it (at least, not when you start on your job.) If he dictates complex sentences that require semi-colons, you'll have to be able to punctuate them perfectly.

For this reason, you will have to study rules on the use of the semi-colon. However, always remember the primary rule:

Wherever possible use a PERIOD rather than a semi-colon.

Rule 1.

Use the semi-colon to separate two related complete thoughts not connected by a conjunction such as **and** *or* **but.**

Our sales have been increasing every day; our competitors' sales have fallen.
This is a fine day; it should not rain before evening.

RULE 2.

A semi-colon precedes an introductory expression such as namely, viz., that is, i.e., for example, e.g.

> The ancients thought there were only four elements; namely, water, earth, air, and fire.
>
> There are numerous potential locations; e.g., Philadelphia, Chicago, Milwaukee.

RULE 3.

Use a semi-colon to separate two long complete thoughts connected by and, but, *or* if *one of these thoughts contains a comma.*

> Having heard of the offer in the newspaper, he rushed to the office; but he found that the job had already been filled.

RULE 4.

Use a semi-colon where commas might be confusing.

> Here are the totals: 6,549; 8,787; and 642,972.

Remember, whenever possible, use a period rather than a semi-colon. In other words, rather have two short sentences than one long sentence that requires a semi-colon. Go back over the example-sentences in this unit on the semi-colon. Do you see how you could break each of them up into more than one sentence by using a period rather than a semi-colon?

For example:

> Our sales have been increasing every day. Our competitors' sales have fallen.
>
> This is a fine day. It should not rain.
>
> Having heard of the offer in the newspaper, he rushed to the office. He found that the job had already been filled.

7. Quotation Marks (" ")

RULE 1.

Use quotation marks to enclose a direct quotation.

> John said, "Take a chance."

NOTE 1. Use quotation marks only around direct quotations.

> RIGHT: He advised me, "Don't get nervous. Just do your job well."
> RIGHT: He advised me not to get nervous but to do my job well.

NOTE 2. When a single quotation is interrupted write it as follows:

> He advised me, "Don't get nervous." He went on to say, "Just do your job well."
> "Send us the bill," he said, "and we will mail you a check by return mail."

NOTE 3. When recording the direct conversation of two or more persons place the statements of each person in separate quotation marks and in separate paragraphs.

> The chairman shouted, "Order! Order in the house!"
> "I will not be silenced," answered Jones, jumping from his seat with arms waving wildly.
> "Gentlemen," interrupted Brown, "let us look at this matter in a calmer frame of mind."

NOTE 4. If a quotation consists of more than one sentence the quotation marks go at the beginning and at the end of the entire statement. If the single quotation consists of more than one paragraph, the quotation marks go at the beginning of each paragraph but at the end of *only* the *last* paragraph.

> The letter read: "We are making this offer just this week. Note that it is being made together with our sale of daytime dresses. We are sure you will like our selection.
> "Any time during the morning that is best for you will be best for us. Will you come?"

NOTE 5. Use single quotation marks to indicate a quotation within a quotation.

> He said, "I believe in the old saying, 'Haste makes waste.'"

RULE 2.

Use quotation marks around the titles of books, magazines and articles.

> Send four copies of "Bookkeeping Made Easy" and four more of "How to Fix It."
> Read the article, "Finland: Land of Opportunity."

It is permissible to set off the title of a book or article without using quotation marks.

1. You may *underline* the title:

Get a copy of Harper's.
We will be pleased to send our folder entitled <u>Become A Stenographer.</u>

2. You may write the title in all-capitals.

Get a copy of HARPER'S.

RULE 3.

Use the quotation marks around unusual words, coined-phrases, or colloquial expressions.

Our sales staff must be "on-the-ball."
We feel that Mr. Jones is a "square-shooter."
The way to understand this problem is to "conceptualize" it in your mind.

RULE 4.

Quotation Marks and other punctuation. Here's where a lot of trouble arises. Learn these simple rules:

1. Always place a final period or comma inside the quotation marks.

He said, "Let the chips fall."
"Give me the figures," Jones said, "and I'll have the answer in a minute."

2. When the entire quotation asks a question, place the question mark *inside* the quotation marks.

He asked, "Who will be kind enough to come to my aid?"

3. When the entire sentence asks a question and the quotation is merely incidental, place the question mark *outside* the quotation marks.

Who has read, "How to Invest"?
Did you receive our booklet, "The Higher Light"?

8. The Apostrophe (')
RULE 1.

Use the apostrophe to indicate the omission of a letter or letters in a contraction.

Can't, won't, wouldn't, they're, you'll, haven't, it's, *etc.*

You don't have the time to go.
Can't you see that we're busy?

It's a fine day.

RULE 2.

Use the apostrophe to form the possessive form of nouns. Review Lesson 2, on *nouns,* now.

> The teacher's success depends in part upon the student's willingness to learn.
> John's office called.
> Stenographers' skills will determine their success.

Remember, as you learned in Chapter 3 on *pronouns:* The possessive form of a pronoun does not take an apostrophe: **hers, its, ours, yours, theirs.**

> Is this book hers?
> Yours truly,
> The firm sent <u>its</u> representative.

It's is a contraction of **it is.**

> It's a fine day.
> <u>We</u> think it's not going to last.

RULE 3.

Use the apostrophe to form the plural of letters and numbers.

> Mississippi has four i's, four s's and two p's.
> This month we ordered a new shipment of No. 105's.

9. The Hyphen (-)

RULE 1.

Use the hyphen to divide a word at the end of a line:

> He thought that it would be too dif-
> ficult.

You may not divide a word in any way you please. There are set rules which you must always observe.

    a. Divide words only between syllables. Therefore a one-syllable word may not be divided.

    b. A two-syllable word may not be divided if one of the syllables consists of only one letter. The word **consists** may be divided into **con-sists.** The word **above** may not be divided into **a-bove.**

c. When a medial syllable of a word is a single vowel, that single vowel should *end* the first line and not start the second. The word **hesitate** consists of the three syllables **hes-i-tate.** It should always be broken down as **hesi-tate,** *not* **hes-itate.**

d. Never divide the last word on a page.

RULE 2.

There are certain expressions that should *always* be hyphenated:

a. Compound words that begin with **self,** such as: **self-conscious, self-evident, self-assurance, self-respect, self-confident.**

b. Compound words that begin with **ex, pro,** or **anti.**
For example: **ex-President, ex-Senator, pro-American, pro-United Nations, anti-Communist.**

c. Compound numbers, such as **fifty-first, fifty-second.**

RULE 3.

There are other expressions that are sometimes hyphenated and sometimes not—expressions such as: **up-to-date, high-class, first-rate, high-grade, well-informed.**

As a rule of thumb, follow this procedure: Whenever any expression such as these comes *directly before* the noun it modifies, it should be hyphenated.

> We have an **up-to-date** *sytem.*
> Our store caters to a **high-class** *clientele.*
> We deal in **first-rate** *goods.*
> We have only **high-grade** *merchandise* that defies comparison.
> He is a **well-informed** *citizen.*

However, when the noun being modified does *not* follow directly, use *no* hyphens.

> Our *system* is **up to date.**
> Our *clientele* is **high class.**
> Our *goods* are **first rate.**
> Our *merchandise* is **high grade** and defies comparison.
> *He* is **well informed** on world affairs.

10. The Parentheses ( )

RULE 1.

Use parentheses to enclose expressions which are incidental, explanatory, or supplementary to the main thought.

> There is no possibility (so I am told) that this deal will be consummated.
> You have already learned (see Lesson 2) about nouns.

RULE 2.

Use parentheses to set off a number which follows the same amount written out.

> We are shipping three hundred (300) tons of Number Two (No. 2) pine board.

NOTE 1. When a sentence ends with an expression in parentheses place the period after the parentheses.

> We can supply the goods for eighty-seven.dollars (87.00).

NOTE 2. When the entire sentence is in parentheses, place the period inside the parentheses.

> The goods must be delivered by Tuesday. (John, please don't let us down.)
> We shall expect shipment at that time.

NOTE 3. Observe the placement of the comma in this sentence:

> To establish fellowship among all men (which is our objective), we must all do our parts.

NOTE 4. In many instances it is proper to use dashes or parentheses, whichever you prefer.

> Right: This offer (and it is our final offer) is too good to be refused.
> Right: This offer—and it is our final offer—is too good to be refused.

11. The Dash (—)

RULE 1.

Use the dash to indicate a break in the continuity of thought.

> The large house—and make no mistake, it was large—was completely demolished by the fire.
> I know—or should I say, I feel—that you will do well.

RULE 2.

Use the dash to emphasize an explanatory phrase.

> We want to tell you about our product—The Schenley car.
> America—that bastion of democracy—has an obligation to all human beings.

NOTE 1. You make the dash by striking the hyphen on the typewriter twice. Leave no space before or after the dash.

NOTE 2. Properly used, the dash is an effective tool to catch the reader's eye and keep him alert. But, if you use the dash too often you destroy its effectiveness and leave a sloppy, difficult-to-read page. The good writer uses the dash only occasionally, when he wants extra *punch*. It is his *Sunday punch*, not his *left jab*.

12. Capitalization

In Lesson 2 you learned about the capitalization of proper nouns. In that section you learned that you:

1. Capitalize the names of the months of the year and the days of the week.
2. Do not capitalize the names of seasons.
3. Capitalize the name of a direction when it refers to a specific section of the country or the world; but do not capitalize a direction when it refers only to a point on the compass.
4. Capitalize a geographical term such as **river** when it appears as part of the name of a particular river or other geographical designation.
5. Capitalize a word such as **hotel** or **highway** when it appears as part of the name of a particular hotel or highway.
6. Capitalize the title of a particular person, especially when he is a high-ranking official.
7. Capitalize the first letter of each important word in the title of a work of art or literature.

Go back to Lesson 2 right now, and review these rules of capitalization. Only after you have thoroughly refamiliarized yourself with these rules, should you proceed to the further rules on capitalization, below.

8. Capitalize the first word of every sentence. (You should need no special examples of this.)

9. Capitalize the first word of a direct quotation that is a complete sentence.

> He said, "This job must be improved upon."
> "This job," he said, "must be improved upon."

Note, however, that if you are quoting an expression that is not a full sentence, you do not capitalize the first word.

> He said that this job "must be improved upon."

10. Capitalize the first word of each line of poetry.

> "What fairings will ye that I bring?"
> Said the King to his daughters three;
> For I to Vanity Fair am bound,
> Now say what shall they be?"

11. Capitalize amounts when spelled out in formal or legal documents.

> Eighty-seven Dollars and Twenty-four Cents
> Sixty-four Thousand Dollars

12. Capitalize the word **dear** in a salutation when it comes at the beginning. Do *not* capitalize **dear** when it is in the middle of the salutation.

> Dear Sir:
> My dear Sir:
> Dear Mr. Jones:
> My dear Mr. Jones:

13. Capitalize only the first word in the complimentary close of a letter.

> Sincerely yours,
> Yours sincerely,
> Very truly yours,

14. Capitalize nouns or pronouns that refer to God or to holy books.

> Please hand me the Bible on that shelf.
> The Holy Scriptures tell us that God created the world in six days and that He rested on the seventh day.

This finishes your study of the rules of punctuation.

You have learned many rules, but they were not too difficult. Actually, almost all of these rules were merely a review for you.

You certainly knew that a period is placed at the end of a sentence that makes a statement, a question mark is placed after a question, and an exclamation point is placed after an exclamation. You knew that the comma is used to separate items listed in a series, to set off introductory expressions such as *however*, and to set off certain explanatory expressions. You knew that quotation marks are placed before and after a direct quotation, and that the first letter of a sentence must be capitalized. You knew all this, and much more.

All in all, probably three-quarters of the rules in this lesson were completely familiar to you. You applied them automatically without a second thought. However, it is mastery of the other one quarter of these rules that spells the difference between the average, run-of-the-mill stenographer and the highly paid, top-notch secretary.

Do you feel you have fully mastered all the rules of punctuation presented in this lesson?

Do you feel certain that every transcript you hand into your teacher and later to your employer will exhibit perfect punctuation?

Here is the turning point in your secretarial training. If you want to be a superior secretary, make certain that you know the rules of punctuation thoroughly. Review this lesson. Then review it again, if necessary. It won't take long, and it will be well worth the small effort.

Exercise 37
The Period

All periods and some capital letters have been omitted from the following paragraphs. Where a letter should be capitalized, cross out the incorrect small letter and write the capitalized letter above it. Where a period has been omitted, insert a period.

This morning we received a request to submit a bid on the equipment specifications for the new vocational school now being erected in Erie, Pa

Exercise 37 (continued)

it is our policy, as you know, to work only through our regular dealers, we suggest, therefore, that you send a representative to follow up this opportunity for some very good business

we can be very helpful to you in preparing your estimate on the list of hand tools, and we hope you will let us work with you the large machine equipment, of course, is out of our line because of your long experience in this field, we know you will have no trouble in submitting a complete bid

* * *

we appreciate the information that you gave us in your letter of October 17

the purchasing agent for the Board of Education in Erie has given us permission to submit a bid on the equipment list for the new school since the bid must be submitted on or before November 19, it is necessary for us to work rapidly

some time ago you stated that there might be price changes after November 1 while we understand that increasing demands are being placed on the tool industry, still we must request a definite guarantee from your company that the prices in effect now will apply to the Erie school contract if it is awarded to our company

Exercise 38

The Question Mark and Exclamation Point

This problem deals with the correct use of the question mark, the exclamation point, and the period. At the end of each of the following sentences place a question mark, an exclamation point, or a period, whichever is correct.

1. Did you send the letter?
2. Please mail it at once
3. Won't you come in, please
4. Why wasn't it filed at once
5. A fine idea
6. The director asked many questions
7. Who is there
8. I am not sure who filed the letter
9. Will you be kind enough to visit us at your next opportunity
10. Why not take a chance
11. Why
12. Can there be any question about his sincerity
13. That is the $64,000 question
14. Amazing
15. What an amazing discovery

137

Exercise 39
Commas: Separating Items in a Series

This problem involves the use of commas to separate items listed in a series. Insert commas in the following sentences wherever necessary.

1. We will leave by car, rail, or plane on Friday.

2. The successful teacher is friendly alert interesting and self-confident.

3. Our store deals in radios TV sets refrigerators and similar products.

4. We have correspondence from you dated August 3 August 18 September 6 and October 15.

5. You will not be able to resist our newest model when you see its long low streamlined appearance.

6. Newspapers magazines books and periodicals all will be on sale this week.

7. Our rates are $3.00 for a room without bath $4.50 for a room with bath and $8.00 for a suite of two rooms.

8. We deal in state bonds municipal bonds industrial bonds and railroad bonds.

9. We deal in state municipal industrial and railroad bonds.

10. Thirty days hath September April June and November.

11. We sell the finest kerosene benzene and alcohol lamps on the market.

12. The properties available are in Detroit St. Louis Cleveland and New York.

13. For lunch we offer roast beef salad and bread and butter.

14. Our courses include shorthand Business English typewriting and bookkeeping.

15. She gave a stately prim correct appearance.

Exercise 40
Commas: Set off Name of Person Addressed

This problem involves the use of commas to set off the name of a person directly addressed. In some of the following sentences commas have been omitted. Fill in all missing commas. Remember, set a name off with commas only if the named person is being directly addressed.

1. Thank you, Mr. Shaw, for the prompt attention given to our questionnaire.

2. We have directed Mr. James King of our credit department to discuss terms of payment with you.

3. They are being shown this week Mrs. Watson.

Exercise 40 (continued)

4. Mr. Adams we have learned that you will soon accept delivery of a new car.

5. I have looked further Mr. Grover into the Gray Lumber situation.

6. Mr. Martin says that economic conditions will continue to be thoroughly sound.

7. Madam does the approach of warm weather suggest sending your furs to storage?

8. Is it the fault of this store that your account remains inactive Mrs. Wright?

9. Mr. White's inspection of our floor equipment was very helpful.

10. The January sales now being held throughout the store offer you exceptional values Mrs. Hays.

11. Let us know Mrs. Jones your reasons for this decision.

12. We feel certain of our grounds Mr. Jackson.

Exercise 41

Commas: Set off Explanatory Expressions

This problem deals with the use of commas to set off explanatory expressions. Insert commas wherever proper in the following sentences.

1. Our representative from New Orleans, Mr. A. J. Johnson, is in town.

2. Asia the largest of the continents is becoming a major focus of international relations.

3. Our new location the corner of Sixth Avenue and Forty-Second Street is ideal for our type of business.

4. Our attorney Mr. G. A. Blake will call at your office tomorrow.

5. B. H. Brown golf champion of the South won the cup handily.

6. It is my pleasure to introduce H. Colin Phillips our friend and leader.

7. Would you enjoy living in a residential park a veritable winter wonderland of over 500 acres of high healthy beautifully wooded fertile land Mr. Smith?

8. We advise you to see either Mr. R. J. Jones Director of the Bureau or Mr. P. T. Smith his assistant.

9. The speakers were H. George Brittingham Professor of Business English and John Rogers Jr. Professor of American History.

10. The Mississippi America's largest river flows into the Gulf of Mexico.

Exercise 42

Commas: Explanatory Expressions II

A. This problem involves the use of commas to set off explanatory expressions. Each of the following sentences involves an explanatory expression that should be set off with commas. Insert commas wherever proper.

1. This morning we received a report from Mr. Johnson, who is our representative in New York.

2. Wellington chalk which is the best chalk you can get is the most economical for school use.

3. Mr. Howard Clark who is president of the National Savings Association sent a copy of his latest address.

4. Our customers who have been most kind to us will be pleased to hear of our latest plans.

5. The manufacture of this equipment which is the finest ever made is a painstakingly exact process.

6. These lessons which you should study every day will provide fine background for your future work.

B. Each of the following sentences involves an explanatory expression that should NOT be set off with commas because to do so would change the meaning of the sentence. *Underline* each such expression.

1. The man who does a poor job does not last long in business.

2. The advertisement that catches the eye is the one that has a certain "plus."

3. A type of work that satisfies one's desire to serve others is medicine.

4. Water that is stagnant is putrid.

5. Anyone who works hard can succeed.

6. Only those who are geniuses gain acclaim as musicians.

C. Each of the following sentences includes an explanatory expression. Some of these expressions should be set off with commas; some should not. Place commas around those expressions which should be set off. Underline those expressions which should not.

1. Water that does not run rapidly becomes stagnant.

2. Your fall order which we received last week has been filled.

3. The man who runs the fastest wins the race.

4. John Doe who was tried for larceny was acquitted.

5. This work which I feel sure you will enjoy is not very difficult.

6. Deliver only those posters that you consider best as soon as you can.

7. The letter that was sent to him came back unopened.

8. The dress that I think you will like best has not yet arrived.

9. Our book is printed in type that is easy on the eye.

10. That woman who spoke to you at such great length yesterday is back.

11. This business which you have merely sampled these past months can provide ample excitement for a lifetime.

12. A red-headed woman who does not have a fiery temper is a rarity.

13. Mr. Oglethorpe is a man who knows this business inside out.

14. The order which we have been awaiting for weeks was delayed again.

15. He is the man whom I would elect.

Exercise 43
Commas: Set off Additions to a Sentence

A. This problem deals with the use of commas to separate conjunctions such as *therefore* from the body of the sentence. Insert commas wherever proper in the following sentences.

Scoring: 0-1 wrong, Excellent; 2 wrong, Good; 3 or more wrong, Restudy Lesson.

1. It is, however, unnecessary for you to reply at once.

2. Feel free of course to take as much time as you need.

3. Naturally we were shocked to hear of the delay.

4. It is nevertheless imperative that your representative contact us at once.

5. We feel on the other hand that your client is entitled to some minor sort of relief.

6. As we understand the situation the failure was entirely the fault of your agent.

7. To be very frank we were satisfied with neither the lamps the shades nor the fixtures.

8. It is in our opinion impossible to predict the outcome at this moment.

9. This class however is the best we have had.

10. No one naturally can be blamed for such an innocent mistake.

B. This problem deals with the use of commas to set off questions that are added to statements, and opposing ideas beginning with *not*. Insert commas wherever necessary in the following sentences.

Scoring: 0 wrong, Excellent; 1 wrong, Good; 2 or more wrong, Restudy Lesson.

1. You received our catalogue, didn't you?

2. We will send you east not west.

3. It's going to be a banner month isn't it?

4. We shall judge a man by his accomplishments not by his looks.

5. We offered you this line last year didn't we?

6. You can do the job can't you?

7. Look for facts not opinions.

8. In treating employees one should be kind and understanding not rude and impatient.

9. This is easy isn't it?

10. We will travel by plane not train.

Exercise 44
Commas: Set off Quotations

This problem deals with the use of the comma to set off a short, direct quotation. Insert commas in the following sentences wherever necessary.

Scoring: 0 wrong, Excellent; 1 wrong, Good; 2 or more wrong, Restudy Lesson.

1. He said, "This is ridiculous."

2. "We shall not stop fighting" said he "nor shall we retreat an inch."

3. "Why" I asked "doesn't he admit he was wrong?"

4. "This is the worst job I have ever seen" was what he said.

5. I told him "Either you accept our offer or we shall deal elsewhere."

Exercise 45
Commas: Separating Thoughts.

A. This is a review problem on run-on sentences and sentence fragments. Rewrite the following letter, correcting all such sentence errors. Review the material on run-on sentences and sentence fragments in Lesson One.

My dear Miss Green:

The Drake Hotel is a comfortable and well-managed house. Situated on a beautiful piece of land in the hills of Bell Harbor. From the heart of Baltimore it can be reached by train or automobile. In less than an hour. Although it is near the city. It is far enough removed for rest and quiet.

Majestic old trees and attractive walks add to the beauty of the grounds the extensive lawns reach to the shore of Chesapeake Bay fishing and boating are always in season.

We extend to you and your friends. A cordial invitation to visit us.

B. This problem deals with the use of the comma in a sentence that contains two long thoughts connected by a conjunction. Insert commas wherever necessary in the following sentences.

1. Our letters haven't been very serious, but underneath their semi-jesting tone runs the feeling that we will eventually get your business.

2. We wish we could make immediate shipment but the demand has been so strong that orders have piled up.

3. Last year we had the pleasure of sending you one of our publications and we hope that it has proved of value.

4. Booklets and showroom demonstrations are interesting but actual performance on the job is convincing.

5. An excellent pool is available for those who like to swim and for those who like to play golf there is a beautiful 18-hole course.

6. Every lesson in the manual is easy and every principle is outlined in complete detail.

7. We would like to stay for another hour but our train is leaving in ten minutes.

8. Forgive our curiosity but why have we not heard from you?

9. You must pay this bill at once or you will hear from our attorneys.

10. You have not written us for many weeks nor have you bothered to pay your bills.

C. This problem deals with the use of the comma to separate a dependent expression from the main part of a sentence. In *some* of the following sentences commas should be inserted. Insert such commas wherever necessary.

1. Despite our advice, he accepted the offer.

2. Rushing to the rescue he was injured by a falling board.

3. Because of your fine past record we are keeping your account open one more week.

4. Forgetting all he had been told he stood before the audience dumbfounded.

5. While walking down the street last week I met an old friend.

6. We have enjoyed full employment despite the world situation.

7. Despite the world situation we have enjoyed full employment.

8. Realizing his position John resigned.

9. John realizing his position resigned.

10. Mr. Smith despite his vast knowledge did not know the answer.

Review Exercise
The Period, Question Mark, Comma

This is an overall problem dealing with the use of the marks of punctuation you have already studied. Insert commas, periods or question marks wherever necessary in the following letters.

Boston 21, Massachusetts

Gentlemen:

Your letter and the booklet "Live Records" reaches us at a time when our bookkeeping is a matter of real concern This booklet therefore has received our careful attention

Since our office force was reduced last year the marked development of business during the past year has increased the importance of our bookkeeping problem Though we have been considering the use of bookkeeping machines for a long time we are not yet convinced however that such a large outlay of money would result in a satisfactory return Nevertheless something must be done to relieve the pressure which is becoming great of our work

Will you kindly have your representative Mr. Roberts call on Monday May 10 at ten o'clock to discuss arrangements

Very truly yours

*　*　*

Dear Mr. White:

No two men are alike

While one man jumps to a conclusion without careful consideration of all available information another man examines each fact checks every claim and profits from the experience of others then he makes his decision.

Two weeks ago our booklet "Live Records" went out to you after reading it you have of ourse made your decision carefully

May we please help you Booklets and showroom demonstrations are interesting but actual performance on the job is convincing

Mail the enclosed card today and we will place in your store one of the machines that you need.

Sincerely yours

Exercise 46

The Colon and Semi-Colon

A. This problem involves the use of the colon. Insert a colon in each of the following sentences wherever proper.

1. Your order includes: one wooden cabinet, one chair, three metal files, one desk.

2. He is quoted as saying "My only regret is that I have but one life to give for my country."

3. At precisely 456 P. M. our plane departs.

4. Our stock on hand is as follows 3000 #10 envelopes, 2500 #13, and 1500 #17.

5. This is what he said "No amount of money could ever repay you for the fine unselfish job you did on behalf of your nation."

B. This problem involves the use of the semi-colon. Insert a semi-colon in each of the following sentences wherever proper.

1. We have not received your exam as yet; consequently, we have delayed sending your next lesson.

2. This is a fine surprise we were just thinking of you.

3. We have done our best the rest is up to you.

4. There are two reasons for our decision mainly, your determination and your doggedness.

5. To be perfectly frank, I am sorry to see him go but I know you had no alternative.

C. This problem involves the use of the colon, semi-colon, comma, and period. Insert these marks wherever proper in the following sentences.

1. We offer a choice of three models: the stately Classical, the functional Colonial, or the streamlined Modern.

2. Once again we are extending the time however in the future there will be no further extensions

3. Standing up in the Assembly Patrick Henry shouted "Give me liberty or give me death"

4. Mrs. Housewife just mail the enclosed card postage is prepaid

5. Here are the traits that I most admire in a man honesty wisdom and perseverence

6. During the past few months which have been especially hectic I have inspected the following areas the Tennessee Valley the Missouri Valley and the Mississippi Delta

7. Therefore we are pleased to be able to extend this invitation but bear in mind that much as we would prefer that it be otherwise this must be our last offer

8. You Mr Smith have already received our final offer henceforth we shall not bother you again

Exercise 47

Quotation Marks and Other Punctuation

A. This problem deals with the use of quotation marks and other marks of punctuation. Insert all necessary punctuation in the following sentences. Capitalize, where necessary.

1. He told his secretary marie give your full attention to the purchase order.

2. do you manufacture these they asked

3. he spoke with authority saying you may be certain that our firm adheres only to the highest standards of business ethics

4. your book southeast asia has become a best-seller

5. did you receive any compensation for writing the coming battle of congress

6. he asked the question how can we justify our own failure to help them

7. of all the men I know he said none compares with mr jones

8. read about our new school cooler the ad ran it will bring comfort to your home or office

9. the enclosed booklet make your own weather will show you how to maintain your volume of business during summer months

10. how are sales for your book make your own weather

B. Properly punctuate the following passage.

Memorandum to J. P. Roberts:

We received a letter from Modern Offices Inc that reads as follows

Gentlemen We have your letter of June 15 in which you enclosed the specifications for the safe equipment to be installed in the new offices of the Martin Manufacturing Company

We shall be glad to send you pictures and details of Western safes that meet these requirements

It would be more convincing however to have you and your customer visit us in Cleveland May we therefore extend an invitation to you and your customer to come to Cleveland at our expense

Please telephone us when it will be convenient for you and we shall make the hotel reservations

We hope to welcome you soon

Cordially yours

In view of the invitation extended to us in this letter I think we should very seriously consider sending a representative to inspect the Western safes on display

Exercise 48

The Apostrophe

A. This problem deals with the proper use of the apostrophe.

1. (It's, Its) a wonderful opportunity for you.

2. Can this be (yours, your's)?

3. (Your, You're) offer is most interesting.

4. The (women's, womens') coats are in here.

5. (There, They're) are three reasons for this decision.

6. Give them (their, they're) due.

7. (They're, Their) fed up with this type of bickering.

8. Send us a gross of (No. 10s, No. 10's) and a hundred (No. 17s, No. 17's).

9. A (mans, man's) success is measured in terms other than money.

10. The company sent (its, it's) form letter.

1. _It's_

2. _____

3. _____

4. _____

5. _____

6. _____

7. _____

8. _____

9. _____

10. _____

B. This problem deals with the use of the apostrophe in forming possessives and contractions. In the following letter, insert apostrophes wherever necessary.

Dear Miss Roberts:

We cant understand the failure of your firms representative to visit any of our shops during his two weeks visit to our city. Its apparent to us that your sales staff misunderstands my companys position in this city. Were not a small chain of widely separated stores. Ours is a large organization with no two stores more than ten blocks apart. None of our stores is more than a few minutes walk from the center of town.

Our figures for the past half years sales reflect this concentration in our citys prime market area. These sales figures show that ours is a very profitable operation. Ones personal tastes shouldnt influence his decisions in business matters. Hard facts and figures should be the businessmans only criteria.

Well be very much pleased to open our books and records to your firm at your representatives convenience. Wouldnt you be foolish to let this opportunity go by unnoticed. Its not too late to change your mind.

Each of our shops has its own individual management and its own individual personality. All of them are famous for their consistently fine goods—the best in mens womens and childrens clothing.

Were justly proud of the reputation weve established among our towns most respected people. Wont you please accept our invitation to send one of your representatives to inspect our stores and our books. Were looking forward to your reply within a few days time.

Sincerely,

Exercise 49

The Hyphen

A. This problem involves the use of the hyphen to divide words at the end of a line. Assume that each of the following words comes at the end of a line. In the spaces provided write the two parts into which the word should be divided. Consult your dictionary, if necessary.

1. problem   prob-   lem
2. narrate   _____   _____
3. amount   _____   _____
4. hopeful   _____   _____
5. message   _____   _____
6. natural   _____   _____
7. question   _____   _____
8. inert   _____   _____
9. innate   _____   _____
10. legible   _____   _____

B. This problem deals with compound words. Some compound words are written as one word. Others are hyphenated. Still others are written as two separate words. Below is a list of compound words written separately. In the space provided, write them properly.

1. self evident   1. _____ self-evident _____
2. letter head   2. _____
3. ex President   3. _____
4. self control   4. _____
5. vice chairman   5. _____
6. father in law   6. _____
7. all right   7. _____
8. can not   8. _____

9. not withstanding   9. _____

10. real estate   10. _____

11. ex governor   11. _____

12. type written   12. _____

13. editors in chief   13. _____

14. over due   14. _____

15. post card   15. _____

16. self conscious   16. _____

17. any body   17. _____

18. vice president   18. _____

19. no one   19. _____

20. some thing   20. _____

Exercise 50
Parenthesis, Dash, and Hyphen

This problem involves the use of the parenthesis, the dash and the hyphen. Insert all necessary punctuation in the following sentences.

1. It is self-evident (at least, it should be so to a reasonable man) that our economic outlook is brightening.

2. Please look at our advertisement you can find one in this month's issue of the New Era to see what we mean by vibrant layout.

3. You should be able to collect the facts and we mean all the facts with little trouble if you are willing to apply yourself.

4. And the Licensee hereby agrees to pay Licensor on the first day of each month commencing on January the first Nineteen hundred and fifty seven the sum of one hundred dollars $100.00.

5. As you have already learned see Lesson XIV the subject of a sentence should agree in person and number.

6. We are interested I might say extremely interested in the report of our men who attended your factory demonstration.

7. As a result of our long experience never forget we have been in business for over a hundred years we feel it our duty to urge you to reconsider your decision.

8. Our representative Mr. Fred Perry didn't you meet him at our last convention will be glad to assist you in any way possible.

Exercise 51
Capitalization

A. The following paragraph is written without any capital letters. Cross out each small letter that should be capitalized. Write the capital letter above it.

on wednesday, january 17, president james jackson delivered his winter message to stockholders of the apex screen co. in a speech entitled, "meeting the mosquito menace," he explained the firm's expansion into the northwest as part of man's never-ending struggle against the insect kingdom. calling for "a screen on every window," he demanded greater efforts in southern parts of the united states where the mosquito problem was most biting.

B. The following letter is written without any capital letters. Cross out each small letter that should be capitalized. Write the capital letter above it.

mr. john murphy

17 lexington avenue

new york, new york

dear sir:

are you one of the many new york city business men who would like to spend a few days or a month in the country, but whose interests demand your attention daily in the city? the hotel gramatan in the westchester hills, midway between the scenic hudson and long island sound, offers you a most inviting home twenty-eight minutes from grand central terminal, the heart of the shopping and theatre center.

the hotel is of moorish design and the wide spanish balconies encircling it are literally "among the tree tops." it is on the american plan, and the rates are less than the cost of equal accommodations in town: single room and board $ per week and upward, large room and private bath with board for two people, $ per week and upward.

an excellent golf course, eight of the best tennis courts in westchester county, a string of fine saddle horses, good roads for motoring and driving are offered those to whom life in the open has a direct appeal.

walter e. gibson, drama critic of the *new york times,* visited the hotel gramatan in july of last year. upon his return to new york, he wrote the following in his column, *going on in new york*: "the hotel gramatan is one of the finest hotels i have ever visited. its european cooking is tops."

why don't you take a drive up the scenic hutchinson river parkway and visit the gramatan some time this fall?

very respectfully yours,

Review Exercise

Punctuation

This problem deals with capitalization and punctuation. The following letter is written with no punctuation marks and no capital letters. Insert all punctuation marks. Where a letter should be capitalized, cross out that letter and write the capital letter above it.

*R*andall and peck inc.

35 draper avenue

rochester 10 new york

gentlemen

the enclosed booklet make your own weather will show you how to maintain your volume of business through the hot summer months read about our new scott portable cooler that will bring summer comfort to homes offices hospitals and hotels in your city it is an air conditioning unit that is both quiet and beautiful it is almost as easy to install as a radio and it can be moved from room to room and from building to building you cannot afford to overlook this opportunity

one large industrial user of the scott portable cooler wrote us as follows

our plant is located in the south where we face tremendous heat problems during most of the year we had considered installing other air conditioning units but all of them were too expensive then we learned about the scott cooler last spring we ordered one of the scott air conditioners for our executive office and were so satisfied with its superb performance that our purchasing manager was instructed to order scott coolers for the entire plant. i can't recommend the scott cooler too highly

take the advice of this successful business man and the thousands like him try the scott cooler

to help our dealers we have arranged a demonstration at the factory on april 8 and 9 we invite your sales and service managers to attend this meeting at our expense.

very truly yours

151

Lesson 11

WORDS FREQUENTLY CONFUSED

1. **Accede** means *to agree to.*
   Exceed means *more than.*

    > We quickly **acceded** to their request.
    > The crops **exceeded** the best reports.

2. **Accept** means *to take when offered.*
   Except means *to leave out.*

    > The winner of the contest **accepted** the check with many thanks.
    > All of us, **except** the youngest, completed the long walks.

3. **Access** means *availability.*
   Excess means *too much.*

    > The reporter was given **access** to the records.
    > The crops this year are far in **excess** of last year.

4. **Adapt** means *to adjust.*
   Adopt means *to take as one's own.*
   Adept means *skilful.*

    > Sensible people can **adapt** themselves to changing situations.
    > Good shop training makes children **adept** in the use of tools.
    > The Constitution was **adopted** by the convention of the Thirteen Original States in 1787.

5. **Addition** means *the act of adding.*
   Edition means *a printing of a book.*

    > In **addition** to a coat, he carried a raincoat.
    > The first **edition** of the paper appears in the morning.

6. **Affect** means *to influence.*
   Effect means *the outcome or the result.*

    > Did it **affect** the lives of many people?
    > What was the **effect** of atomic energy on civilization?

7. **Adverse** means *unfavorable.*
   Averse means *to dislike.*

    > The batter objected to the **adverse** decision of the umpire.

152

Most students are **averse** to hard study in hot weather.

8. **Advise** means *to give counsel.*

  Advice means *the counsel given.*

   > The lawyer **advised** his client to sign the papers.
   > The client took his **advice.**

9. **Annual** means *yearly.*

  Annul means *to cancel.*

   > The **annual** meeting will be held this Friday.
   > The student council **annulled** the charter of the fraternity for misconduct.

10. **Appraise** means *to set a value.*

  Apprise means *to inform.*

   > The expert **appraised** the painting at a very high value.
   > Paul Revere **apprised** the patriots of the coming of the British.

11. **Assent** means *agreement.*

  Ascent means *climb.*

   > Mr. Smith gave **assent** to my promotion.
   > The **ascent** up the hill was too much for me.

12. **Attain** means *to reach.*

  Attend means *to be present at.*

   > Rosemarie **attained** her great ambition—she **attended** her first prom.

13. **Breath** means *an intake of air.*

  Breathe means *to take air in and out.*

  Breadth means *width.*

   > Take a deep **breath.**
   > Don't **breathe** while swimming under water.
   > The **breadth** of the room is almost as great as its length.

14. **Cease** means *to end.*

  Seize means *to take hold of.*

   > **Cease** that clatter!
   > Run after the dog and **seize** his leash.

15. **Celery** means *a vegetable.*

  Salary means *payment.*

   > Eat your **celery.**
   > Work hard and earn your **salary.**

16. **Cent** means *a coin.*

  Scent means *an odor.*

Sent is the past tense of *send*.

> A **cent** is worth one-tenth of a dime.
> The **scent** of the perfume is fragrant.
> I was **sent** on an errand.

17. **Choice** means *a selection*.

Choose means *to select*.

Chose means *to have selected*.

> Mary's **choice** for a career is stenography.
> We **choose** a President every four years.
> Mary **chose** stenography for her career.

18. **Cite** means *to quote*.

Sight means *seeing*.

Site means *a place for a building*.

> The teacher **cited** a line from the Twenty-Third Psalm.
> My **sight** has declined in my latter years.
> The building is on a prominent **site**.

19. **Close** means *nearby*. (Sounds like: *gross*.)

Close means *to shut*. (Sounds like: *hoze*.)

Clothes means *what we wear*.

Cloths means *fabrics*. (Sounds like: *moths*.)

> I live **close** to the school.
> Please **close** the door.
> The models wore **clothes** to perfection.
> Those **cloths** are really summer material.

20. **Complement** means *to complete*. (Note: *Comple*-ment; *Comple*:te.)

Compliment means *praise*.

> Your new hat **complements** your outfit.
> The pretty girl accepted the **compliments** as usual.

21. **Council** means *an assembly*.

Counsel means *to advise*.

> The premier called a meeting of his **council** of ministers.
> The ministers **counseled** the premier to act swiftly.

22. **Coarse** means *rough*.

Course means *a plan of action or direction*.

> The coat is made of **coarse** cloth.
> The skipper followed a definite **course**.

23. **Decease** means *die; death.*

    Disease means *illness.*

    > The newspaper reported the **decease** of the mayor.
    > Cancer is a deadly **disease.**

24. **Device** means *a way to do a thing.*

    Devise means *to find the way to do a thing.*

    > A corkscrew is a **device** for pulling corks out of bottles.
    > Einstein **devised** a formula for freeing the atom.

25. **Deference** means *respect.*

    Difference means *unlikeness.*

    > Well-bred young people show due **deference** to their parents.
    > The **difference** between the two firms is striking.

26. **Emerge** means *to rise out of.*

    Immerge means *to sink into.*

    > The swimmer **emerged** from the ocean.
    > My laundress completely **immerged** my dress in the sink of water.

27. **Eminent** means *important.*

    Imminent means *about to happen.*

    Emanate means *to come out from.*

    > Many **eminent** men were called to advise the President.
    > Accidents are always **imminent** in heavy traffic, so drive carefully.
    > Queer odors often **emanate** from the chemistry room.

28. **Expand** means *to spread out.*

    Expend means *to use up.*

    > Our school **expanded** its quarters with two new rooms.
    > Don't **expend** all the money you earn.

29. **Fair** means *pretty; light in color; reasonable; a carnival.*

    Fare means *set price.*

    > We do not consider your tactics to be **fair.**
    > Pay your **fare** on the bus.

30. **Feat** means *something done well.*

    Feet is the plural of *foot.*

    > It was quite a **feat** for the six-year old girl to swim thirty yards.
    > There are three **feet** in a yard.

31. **Formally** means *according to set rules.*

    Formerly means *in past time.*

The governor was **formally** sworn into office.

Formerly, a wife had to sue in her husband's name.

32. **Forth** means *forward*.

Fourth is the count after *third*.

> On the **fourth** count, the whole company stepped **forth**.

33. **Hole** means *an opening*.

Whole means *entire*.

> The **hole** in the fence has been mended.
> The **whole** series of books has been revised.

34. **Lessen** means *to make less*.

Lesson means *something to learn*.

> To **lessen** my troubles, I prepared all of my **lessons**.

35. **Miner** means *one who works in a mine*.

Minor means *a person under legal age; unimportant*.

> No **minor** may be employed as a coal **miner**.

36. **Moral** means *good; just; ethical*.

Morale means *spirit*.

> The person of high **moral** standards is a credit to his people.
> The **morale** of a class is high when the teacher has its respect.

37. **Packed** means *full*.

Pact means *a treaty*.

> The hall is **packed** with children.
> The **pact** between the company and the union was signed today.

38. **Pair** means *two of a kind*.

Pare means *to peel*.

Pear means *a fruit*.

> What do you think of this **pair** of shoes.
> It's easy to eat an apple if you **pare** it first.
> A carload of luscious **pears** is being shipped by train.

39. **Pedal** means *a lever moved by foot*.

Peddle means *to sell from door to door*.

> You ride a bicycle by moving the **pedals**.
> No longer do we see things **peddled** from door to door.

40. **Persecute** means *to oppress*.

Prosecute means *to sue in court*.

> Tyrants **persecute** their people to keep themselves in power.

It is the business of the district attorney to **prosecute** all persons accused of crime.

41. **Personal** means *private*.

    Personnel means *the staff*.

    My business with you is purely **personal**.
    The **personnel** director of the firm selects all the employees.

42. **Physic** means *a drug*.

    Physics means *a branch of science*.

    Physique means *body structure*.

    Take a **physic** on a doctor's order.
    Physics is the study of energy and motion.
    The athlete was proud of his **physique**.

43. **Plain** means simple; or *a prairie*.

    Plane means *a flat surface; a tool for smoothing; an airplane*.

    The problem is **plain** to see.
    Smooth the wood by using a **plane**.
    The **airplane** is a modern invention.

44. **Pole** means *a long stick*.

    Poll means *vote*.

    The flag flies at the top of the **pole**.
    The class took a **poll** to see who was the most popular girl.

45. **Principal** means *the most important; the head*.

    Principle means *a truth*.

    The **principal** men of the city met to discuss the new tax bill.
    The **principles** in the Constitution are the bases of our liberties.

46. **Rain** means *water from the clouds*.

    Reign means *rule*.

    Rein means *a strip of leather for guiding a horse*.

    Rain is needed to make plants grow.
    Elizabeth II **reigns** over England.
    Don't draw the **reins** too tight on the horse.

47. **Sail** means *to travel on water; a canvas sheet on a ship*.

    Sale means *selling*.

157

The ships **sail** along with the wind.
A special **sale** is going on at the store.

48. **Scene** means *a view.*

    Seen is the past tense of **see.**

    > What a **scene** from my window!
    > The boy was **seen** running away.

49. **Sole** means *all alone* (from the word, **solo.**)

    Soul means *the spirit of man.*

    > I am the **sole** tenant in the house.
    > The **soul** of man is immortal.

50. **Stake** means *a stick; a wager.*

    Steak means *a slice of beef.*

    > Drive the **stake** into the ground.
    > We broiled the **steak** on the flames.

51. **Stationary** means *standing still.*

    Stationery means *paper for writing.*

    (Note: The suffix **ary** means *relating to.* It is easy to remember that **stationary** means *relating to* something standing or fixed.)

    > The sign at the crossing is **stationary.**
    > We use good **stationery** in our office.

52. **Steal** means *to take another's property.*

    Steel means *a metal made from iron.*

    > To take someone else's property unlawfully is to **steal** it.
    > The knife is of the finest **steel.**

53. **Tear** means *water from the eyes.* (Note: Sounds like, **mere.**)
    Tear means *to rip apart.* (Note: Sounds like, **air.**)
    Tier means *row.* (Note: Sounds like, **mere.**)

    > The **tears** dropped from her eyes.
    > **Tear** up that letter and throw the pieces away.
    > In that stadium, there are many **tiers** of seats.

54. **Their** means *belonging to them.*

    There means *in that place.*

    They're is a contraction of, **they are.**

They're very fine people, and their home shows it.
If he won't come here, I'll go there.

55. **Thorough** means *complete.*

    Threw is the past tense of **throw.**

    Through means *into and beyond.*

    > The maid cleaned the room **thoroughly.**
    > The pitcher **threw** a beautiful curve.
    > I went **through** the tunnel.

56. **Vain** means *proud in a silly way.*

    Vane means *a device on a steeple which shows which way the wind blows.*

    Vein means *a blood vessel.*

    > Why be **vain** of your beauty?
    > The old barn still has a **vane** on the roof.
    > **Veins** carry blood to the heart.

57. **Waist** means *a part of the body.*

    Waste means *to dissipate.*

    > In that dress she has a narrow **waist.**
    > We must not **waste** water during a drought.

58. **Ware** means *something to sell.*

    Wear means *to have on.*

    > The peddler sells his **wares**—potware, silverware, and copperware.
    > You may **wear** my new hat.

59. **Waive** means *to give up.*

    Wave means *a swell of water.*

    > When the partners separated, one of them **waived** all claims to any of the property.
    > Watch the **waves** rise and fall.

60. **Weather** means *the state of the climate.*

    Whether means *a choice.*

    > In spring, we expect good **weather.**
    > **Whether** or not we go depends upon the **weather.**

Exercise 52

Words Frequently Confused I

In the space provided, write the correct word.

1. General Cornwallis (acceded, exceeded) to Washington's terms.   1. ___acceded___
2. The results (accede, exceed) my wildest expectations.   2. _____
3. I cannot (accept, except) your offer.   3. _____
4. Everyone attended the banquet (accept, except) Mr. Smith.   4. _____
5. Do you have (access, excess) to the stockroom?   5. _____
6. There is an (access, excess) of coffee in the market at present.   6. _____
7. A carpenter must be completely (adapt, adept, adopt) with all his tools.   7. _____
8. It will be easy for him to (adapt, adept, adopt) himself to college life.   8. _____
9. This (addition, edition) of Shakespeare's works will be a valuable (addition, edition) to your library.   9. _____ _____
10. What is the (affect, effect) of heat upon water?   10. _____
11. How does heat (affect, effect) water?   11. _____
12. All sensible men are (averse, adverse) to war.   12. _____
13. The new law may have an (adverse, averse) effect upon business.   13. _____
14. Why should I (advice, advise) people who have no interest in taking my (advice, advise)?   14. _____ _____
15. At the (annual, annul) meeting of the national organization, they may (annual, annul) the charter of the local chapter.   15. _____ _____
16. We cannot (appraise, apprise) the value of this property until we have been (appraised, apprised) of all relevant facts.   16. _____ _____
17. Are you sure the authorities will give their (ascent, assent) to your making the (ascent, assent) up the mountain?   17. _____ _____
18. Holding his (breath, breathe, breadth), he swam, without coming to the surface, the entire (breath, breathe, breadth) of the pool.   18. _____ _____
19. He (ceased, seized) the opportunity to shout his disapproval.   19. _____
20. Unless you (cease, seize) shipping the goods at once, our   20. _____

160

orders are to (cease, seize) all outgoing shipments.   _____

21. It is (two, to, too) late to call him now.   21. _____

22. What a fragrant (cent, scent, sent)!   22. _____

23. I would not offer you a (cent, scent, sent) for your scheme. 23. _____

24. Our (choice, choose, chose) for president is a man I am sure 24. _____

    you all will want to (choice, choose, chose).   _____

25. I (cite, sight, site) Mr. Daniel Webster as my authority in 25. _____

    the case.

26. My (cite, sight, site) is so poor that I cannot read without 26. _____

    glasses.

27. That corner would be a good (cite, sight, site) for a bank. 27. _____

28. Before you leave please (cloths, clothes, close) the door   28. _____

    of the (cloths, clothes, close) closet.   _____

29. We wish to (complement, compliment) you upon your fine   29. _____

    work.

30. A battleship's (complement, compliment) includes over two   30. _____

    thousand men.

Exercise 53

Words Frequently Confused II

In the space provided to the right of each choice, write the correct word.

1. The President sought the (council, counsel) of his cabinet in 1. _____

   the matter.

2. The Student (Council, Counsel) rules on all student problems. 2. _____

3. When the time comes, we will know what (coarse, course)   3. _____

   to follow.

4. This (cloth, clothes, close) has a very (coarse, course) texture. 4. _____

   _____

5. Measles is a childhood (decease, disease).   5. _____

6. I read of his (decease, disease) in the obituary column.   6. _____

7. Can you (device, devise) an easy way to fix this lock?

7. _____

8. It is a very complicated (device, devise).

8. _____

9. They speak of him with great reverence and (deference, difference).

9. _____

10. The (deference, difference) between eight and ten is two.

10. _____

11. The submarine (emerged, immerged) out of the water.

11. _____

12. The white whale, (emerged, immerged) into the depths of the ocean.

12. _____

13. This broadcast (emanates, eminents, imminents) from Radio City.

13. _____

14. When one drives at such speed, danger is always (emanate, eminent, imminent).

14. _____

15. Matter (expands, expends) when heated.

15. _____

16. We have (expanded, expended) too much money on this project.

16. _____

17. The subway (fair, fare) is fifteen cents.

17. _____

18. It is a (fair, fare) question.

18. _____

19. I consider it a remarkable (feat, feet) for an athlete to broad jump over twenty (feat, feet).

19. _____
_____

20. Everyone at the ball was (formerly, formally) attired.

20. _____

21. They (formally, formerly), gave such mortgages only to veterans.

21. _____

22. This is the (forth, fourth) time we have had this same trouble.

22. _____

23. The men stepped (forth, fourth) when their names were called.

23. _____

24. You must tell the truth, the (hole, whole) truth, and nothing but the truth.

24. _____

25. The explosion ripped a (hole, whole) three (feat, feet) wide.

25. _____

Exercise 54

Words Frequently Confused III

In the space provided, write the correct word.

1. The hall was (packed, pact) with dignitaries who came to watch the signing of the North Atlantic (Packed, Pact).

1. _____
   _____

2. How much is this (pair, pare, pear) of shoes?

2. _____

3. Mrs. Jones had to (pair, pare, pear) all the (pairs, pares, pears) before she could cook them.

3. _____
   _____

4. The (pedal, peddle) on the bicycle is broken.

4. _____

5. We do not intend to (pedal, peddle) our wares from door to door.

5. _____

6. The early Christian martyrs were often (persecuted, prosecuted).

6. _____

7. The District Attorney (persecutes, prosecutes) all suspects indicted by the state.

7. _____

8. The (personal, personnel) in our office have been carefully selected.

8. _____

9. May I ask you a (personal, personnel) question?

9. _____

10. The (plain, plane) landed at the airport despite the fog.

10. _____

11. The carpenter used his (plain, plane) to smooth out the door.

11. _____

12. It is (plain, plane) to see that he is better.

12. _____

13. The telephone company is slowly replacing its (poles, polls) in this block.

13. _____

14. Will the clerk please (pole, poll) the Senators to recheck the vote.

14. _____

15. The basic (principals, principles) of Relativity are not understood by all men.

15. _____

16. The (principal, principle) of my high school is not respected in our community.

16. _____

17. The (rain, reign, rein) of Elizabeth will be long and   17. _____
    peaceful.

18. The cowboy gripped the (rains, reigns, reins) as he led his   18. _____
    horse over the rocks made slippery by the (rain, reign, rein).   _____

19. The mayor (thorough, threw, through) out the first ball.   19. _____

20. The (vain, vane, vein) person is most often disliked.   20. _____

21. The miners struck a rich (vain, vane, vein) of gold.   21. _____

22. The weather (vain, vane, vein) indicated a strong wind.   22. _____

23. She has (waisted, wasted) most of her fortune on impractical   23. _____
    deals.

24. Her (waist, waste) is so small you could put your two hands   24. _____
    around it.

25. Do you think he charges a fair price for his (wares, wears)?   25. _____

26. She (wares, wears) exquisite clothes.   26. _____

27. We, hereby, (waive, wave) all rights to this property.   27. _____

28. It all depends upon the (weather, whether).   28. _____

COMMON ABBREVIATIONS

1. States and Territories:

Alabama	Ala.	Nebraska	Nebr.
Alaska	Alaska	Nevada	Nev.
Arizona	Ariz.	New Hampshire	N. H.
Arkansas	Ark.	New Jersey	N. J.
California	Calif.	New Mexico	N. Mex.
Colorado	Colo.	New York	N. Y.
Connecticut	Conn.	North Carolina	N. C.
Delaware	Del.	North Dakota	N. Dak.
District of	D. C.	Ohio	Ohio
Columbia		Oklahoma	Okla.
Florida	Fla.	Oregon	Oreg.
Georgia	Ga.	Pennsylvania	Pa.
Guam	Guam	Puerto Rico	P. R.
Hawaii	Hawaii *	Rhode Island	R. I.
Idaho	Idaho	Samoa	Samoa
Illinois	Ill.	South Carolina	S. C.
Indiana	Ind.	South Dakota	S. Dak.
Iowa	Iowa	Tennessee	Tenn.
Kansas	Kans.	Texas	Tex.
Kentucky	Ky.	Utah	Utah
Louisiana	La.	Vermont	Vt.
Maine	Maine	Virginia	Va.
Maryland	Md.	Virgin Islands	V. I.
Massachusetts	Mass.	Washington	Wash.
Michigan	Mich.	West Virginia	W. Va.
Minnesota	Minn.	Wisconsin	Wis.
Mississippi	Miss.	Wyoming	Wyo.
Missouri	Mo.		
Montana	Mont.		

* T. H. (Territory of Hawaii)
is also used.

2. Canadian Provinces:

Alberta	Alta.	Nova Scotia	N.S.
British Columbia	B.C.	Ontario	Ont.
Manitoba	Man.	Prince Edward Island	P.E.I.
New Brunswick	N.B.	Quebec	Que.
Newfoundland	Nfld.	Saskatchewan	Sask.

3. Months of the Year:

Jan.	January	July	July
Feb.	February	Aug.	August
Mar.	March	Sept.	September
Apr.	April	Oct.	October
May	May	Nov.	November
June	June	Dec.	December

4. Compass Directions.

E.	East	S.	South
N.	North	S.E.	Southeast
N.E.	Northeast	S.W.	Southwest
N.W.	Northwest	W.	West

5. Units of Measure:

Length

c.m	centimeter
ft.	foot, feet
in.	inch
m.	meter
mi.	mile
mm.	millimeter
yd.	yard

Weight

cg.	centigram
gm.	gram
gr.	grain
kg.	kilogram
lb.	pound
mg.	milligram
oz.	ounce

Time

d.	day
hr.	hour
min.	minute
mo.	month
sec.	second
yr.	year
a.m.	before noon
M.	noon
p.m.	after noon

Electronic

a.	ampere
c.	cycle
kc.	kilocycle
kv.	kilovolt
kw.	kilowatt
mc.	megacycle
v.	volt
w.	watt

6. Standard Business Terms:

@	At	Ea.	Each
Admr.	Administrator	Ed.	Editor
Admx.	Administratrix	e.g.	for example
A. D.	In the year of our Lord	Elec.	Electric
		Empl.	Employment
Advt., Ad.	Advertisement	Enc., Encl.	Enclosure
Agmt.	Agreement	Esq.	Esquire
Agt.	Agent	Et al.	And others
Ann.	Annual	Etc.	(Et cetera) and so forth
Anon.	Anonymous		
Ans.	Answer	Ex., Exch.	Exchange
Approx.	Approximately	Exec.	Executor
Art.	Article	Execx.	Executrix
Assn.	Association	Exp.	Expense, Express
Att., Atty.	Attorney	Ext.	Extension
Av., Avg.	Average	F., Fahr.	Fahrenheit
Bal.	Balance	Fig.	Figure
B. C.	Before Christ	f.o.b.	Free on board
Bdl.	Bundle	Fr.	French
Bds.	Boards	Frt., Fgt.	Freight
B/L	Bill of Lading	Fwd.	Forward
Bldg.	Building	Gal.	Gallon
B/P, B. Pay.	Bills payable	Gen., Gen'l	General
B/R, B. Rec.	Bills receivable	G. F. A.	General Freight Agent
B/S	Bill of Sale		
Bro.	Brother	Gov.	Governor
Bros.	Brothers	Gov't	Government
Bu.	Bushel	Gr.	Gross
Cap.	Capital	h.p.	Horsepower
Capt.	Captain	I. B.	Invoice Book
C/B	Cash Book	Ibid.	In the same place
Chap.	Chapter	i.e.	That is
Chg.	Charge	Impr.	Improvement
Co.	Company, County	Inc.	Incorporated, Income
c.o.d.	Collect (cash) on delivery		
		Ins.	Insurance
Col.	Colonel	Int.	Interest
Com.	Commerce	Inv.	Invoice, Investment
Comm.	Commission, Committee		
		Invt.	Inventory
Cons.	Consolidated, Consolidation	Ital.	Italics
		Journ.	Journal
Corp.	Corporation	J. P.	Justice of the Peace
C. P. A.	Certified Public Accountant		
		Jr.	Junior
Cr.	Creditor	Lat.	Latitude
Cts.	Cents	Lieut., Lt.	Lieutenant
Cum.	Cumulative	L.f.	Ledger folio
Cwt.	Hundredweight	L. P.	List Price
Deg.	Degree	Ltd.	Limited
Dept.	Department	M	Thousand
Dis., Disc.	Discount	Maj.	Major
Dist.	District	Mdse.	Merchandise
Div.	Division, Dividend	Memo., Mem.	Memorandum
Dol.	Dollar		
Doz.	Dozen	Messrs.	Messieurs
Dr.	Doctor, Debtor	Mfg.	Manufacturing
Dwt.	Pennyweight	Mfr.	Manufacturer

Mgr.	Manager	Qt.	Quart
Misc.	Miscellaneous	Rec.	Receivable
Mme.	Madame	Rec't	Receipt
Mmes.	Mesdames	Ref.	Reference
M. O.	Money Order	Reg.	Regular,
Mr.	Mister		Registered
Mrs.	Mistress	Reorg.	Reorganization
Ms.	Manuscript	Rep't	Report
Mt.	Mount	R. F. D.	Rural free delivery
Nat., Nat'l	National	Rev. a/c	Revenue account
N. B.	Note well	Rm.	Room
No., #	Number	R. R.	Railroad
N. P.	Notary Public	Ry.	Railway
N.S.F., N/S	Not Sufficient	Sav. Bks.	Savings Banks
	Funds	Sec., Sec'y	Secretary
O. D.	Overdraft	Sect.	Section
O. K.	All right, Correct	Shpt.	Shipment
Org.	Organization	Sq.	Square
Orig.	Original	Sr.	Senior
P.	Page	S. S.	Steamship
Pac.	Pacific	Subsid.	Subsidiary
Par.	Paragraph	Supp.	Supplement
Pc.	Piece, Pieces	Supt., Sup't	Superintendent
Pd.	Paid	Synd.	Syndicate
Pfd.	Preferred (stock)	T/B	Trial Balance
Pkg.	Package	Tel.	Telephone,
Plff.	Plaintiff		Telegraph
P & L, P/L	Profit and Loss	Tr.	Trust, Trustee
P. M.	Postmaster	Treas.	Treasurer
P. O.	Post Office	Twp.	Township
Pp.	Pages	Univ.	University
Pr.	Pair	Via	By way of
Pres.	President	Viz.	Namely
Prin.	Principal	Vol.	Volume
Prof.	Professor	Vs.	Against
P. S.	Postscript	Wk.	Week
Pt.	Pint, Part	W/B	Way Bill
Pub.	Publishing,	W. R.	Warehouse Receipt
	Publisher	Wt.	Weight
Qr.	Quire, Quarter		

APPENDIX

INDEX

A

A (Indefinite Article) 72, 77, 78
Accede, Exceed 152
Access, Excess 152
Action Verbs 38-40, 58, 80, 85, 105
Addition, Edition 152
Addresses—Use of Comma 125
Adapt, Adopt, Adept 152
Adjectives 67-78
  Articles 72, 77, 78
  Choosing between adjectives and
    adverbs 80, 85-86
  Comparison (Comparative and
    Superlative Degrees 67-69,
    74-75
  Formation of adverbs 79, 84
  Good-Well 81, 86
  Real-Really 87
Adverbs 79-87
  Choosing between adjectives and
    adverbs 80, 85-86
  Double Negatives 82
  Formation 79, 84
  Good-Well 81, 86
  Most-Almost 82, 87
  Real-Very 83; Real-Really 87
Adverse, Averse 152
Advise, Advice 153
Affect, Effect 152
Agreement of Pronouns with Ante-
  cedents 32-35, 36-37
Agreement of Subject and Predicate
  8-13, 17
Almost-Most 82, 87
Among-Between 89, 93

An 72, 77
And, But—use of comma to sepa-
  rate two independent clauses
  123
Annual, Annul 153
Antecedents—agreement of pro-
  nouns 32-35, 36-37
Anybody 11
Apostrophe, Use of 130
Appraise, Apprise 153
As-Than 100; As-Like 113, 114
Assent, Ascent 153
Attain, Attend 153

B

Be 39
Between-Among 89, 93
Between you and me 101
Breath, Breathe, Breadth 153
But, And—Use of comma to sepa-
  rate two independent clauses
  123

C

Capitalization 19-22, 27, 134-135
Cease, Seize 153
Celery, Salary 153
Cent, Scent 153
Choice, Choose, Chose 154
Choosing between Adjectives and
  Adverbs 80, 85-86
Cite, Sight, Site 154
Close, Clothes, Cloths 154
Coarse, Course 154
Colon, Use of 126

Comma 117-126
  Expressions explaining preceding
    word 119-121
  Use before *and* and *but* 123
  Use in complimentary close of
    letters 125
  Use in dependent clauses 125
  Use in quotations 123
  Use with proper nouns, dates,
    addresses etc. 125
Comparative Degree of Adjectives
  67-69, 74-75
Complement, Compliment 154
Complimentary Close in Letters—
  use of comma 125
Compound Nouns 24
Conjunctions 7, 112-114
  Like-As 113, 114
  Provided-Providing 113, 114
  Try and ... 113, 114
Council, Counsel 154

D

Dates—use of comma 125
Decease, Disease 155
Deference, Difference 155
Dependent Clauses 5; Punctuation
  124
Device, Devise 155
Double Negatives 82

E

Each 11
Each Other 71, 76
Emerge, Immerge 155
Eminent, Imminent, Emanate 155
Exclamation Point 117
Expand, Expend 155

F

Fair, Fare 155
Feat, Feet 155
Fewer-Less 70, 75
First-Last 70

Formally, Formerly 155
Formation of Adverbs 79, 84
Forth, Fourth 156
From-Than 89
Future Perfect Tense 44
Future Tense 40

G

Good-Well 81, 86
Groups used as subject 13

H

Hole, Whole 156
Hyphen 131

I

If I were 57, 65
In-Into 89, 93
Interjections 113
Into-In 89, 93
Irregular and Regular Verbs 48-52,
  60-63
Its-It's 31, 131

L

Last-First 70
Lay-Lie 53-55, 64
Less-Fewer 70, 75
Lessen, Lesson 156
Lie-Lay 53-55, 64
Like-As 113, 114
Linking Verbs 38-40, 58, 80, 85, 98,
  105, 107
Lump Sums (tons, miles etc.) used
  as subject 12

M

Most-Almost 82, 87

N

Negatives, Double 82
News, used as subject 12

Nobody 11
Nouns 18-29
    Capitalization of proper nouns
        19-22, 27, 134-135
    Plural form 22-25
    Compound Nouns 24
    Possessive Nouns 25-26
    Number, used as subject 13

O

Objective Pronouns 98, 106, 108-110
Objects of Verbs 52-53, 63
Objects of Prepositions 88
Of-Off 89, 93
Off-Of 89, 93
One Another 71, 76
Only, placement in sentence 71, 76

P

Packed, Pact 156
Pair, Pare, Pear 156
Parentheses 133
Parts of the Sentence 1
Past Perfect Tense 42-44, 59
Past Tense 40
Pedal, Peddle 156
Perfect Tenses of Verbs 42-46
Period, Use of 115, 127
Persecute, Prosecute 156
Personal, Personnel 157
Physic, Physics, Physique 157
Plain, Plane 157
Plural Form of Nouns 22-25, 27-29
Pole, Poll 157
Possessive Nouns 25-26, 29
Possessive Pronouns 30-31
Predicate 2, 8
Prepositions 11, 88-96
    Objects of prepositions 88
    Right preposition 90-96
    Unnecessary prepositions 90
Present Perfect Tense 44-46, 60
Present Tense 40
Principal, Principle 157

Progressive Form of Verbs 41-42, 59
Pronouns 30-37, 97-111
    Antecedents (agreement with)
        32-35, 36-37
    Objective pronouns 98, 106,
        108-110
    Possessive pronouns 30-31, 35,
        106
    Relative pronouns 31-32
    Us-We 100, 106-110
    Who-Whom 101, 110
    Whoever-Whomever 104, 110
Proper Nouns 10-22, 27, 134
Provided, Providing 113, 114
Punctuation 115-151
    Apostrophe 130
    Capitalization 19-22, 27, 134-135
    Colon 126
    Comma 117-126
        Expressions explaining preced-
            ing word 119-121
        Use in quotations 122
        Use before *and* and *but* 123
        Use in dependent clauses 124
        Use with proper nouns, dates,
            addresses etc. 125
        Use in complimentary close of
            letters 125
    Dash 133
    Exclamation point 117
    Hyphen 131
    Parentheses 133
    Period 115, 127
    Semicolon 127
    Question mark 116
    Quotation marks 128-130

Q

Quotation Marks 128-130
Quotations, Direct and Indirect—
    punctuation 123

R

Rain, Reign, Rein 157
Raise-Rise 56-57, 65

Real-Very 83; Real-Really 87
Regular and Irregular Verbs 48-52,
    60-63
Relative Pronouns (Who, Which,
    That) 31-32
Repetition of Definite Article 73, 78
Rise-Raise 56-57, 65
Run-On Sentences 6, 15, 16, 124

S

Sail, Sale 157
Scene, Seen 158
Semicolon, Use of 127
Sentence, Definition 1, 6
Sentence Fragments 3, 14, 16, 125
Set-Sit 55-56, 64
Simple Tenses (Present, Past,
    Future) 40
Sit-Set 55-56, 64
Sole, Soul 158
Stake, Steak 158
Stationary, Stationery 158
Steal,Steel 158
Subject of Sentence 2, 8-13, 14, 98
Summary of Verb Tenses 46
Superlative Degree of Adjectives
    68-69, 74-75

T

Tear, Tier 158
Than-From 89; Than-As 100
That-This 70
That, Who, Which (Relative Pro-
    nouns) 31-32
The 72, 73, 78
Their, There, They're 158
Them 70
This-That 70
Thorough, Threw, Through 159
Try and 113, 114

U

Unnecessary Prepositions 90
Us-We 100, 106-110

V

Vain, Vane, Vein 159
Verb Forms (Principal Parts)
    47-52
Verbs 38-66
    Action and linking verbs 38-40,
        58, 80, 85, 105
    Direct objects 52-53, 63
    If I were 57, 65
    Lie-Lay, Sit-Set, Rise-Raise
        53-56, 64-65
    Perfect tenses (Present perfect,
        Past perfect, Future perfect)
        42-46, 59-60
    Progressive form 41-42, 59
    Regular and irregular verbs
        48-52, 60-63
    Simple tenses (Present, Past,
        Future) 40
    Summary of tenses 46
    Verb forms (principal parts)
        47-52
    Verb *to be* 39
Very-Real 83

W

Waist, Waste 159
Waive, Wave 159
Ware, Wear 159
Was-Were 57, 65
We-Us 98, 106-110
Weather, Whether 159
Well-Good 81, 86
Were-Was 57, 65
Which, Who, That (Relative Pro-
    nouns) 31-32
Who, Which, That (Relative Pro-
    nouns) 31, 32
Who-Whom 101, 110
Whoever-Whomever 104, 110
Whom-Who 101, 110
Whomever-Whoever 104, 110
Words Frequently Confused
    152-164

174

NOTES

NOTES

NOTES

NOTES

NOTES

NOTES

NOTES

NOTES